CITY DOG

CITY DOG

ESSAYS

W. S. Di PIERO

Northwestern University Press • Evanston, Illinois

Northwestern University Press
www.nupress.northwestern.edu

Printed in the United States of America

10   9   8   7   6   5   4   3   2   1

Library of Congress Cataloging-in-Publication Data

Di Piero, W. S.
    City dog : essays / W. S. Di Piero.
        p. cm.
    Collection of essays, some previously published.
    ISBN 978-0-8101-2516-2 (pbk. : alk. paper)
    1. Di Piero, W. S.—Biography. 2. Poets, American—20th century—Biography.
I. Title.
PS3554.I65C57 2009
814.54—dc22

                                                                    2008048252

To Nikki Martin

CONTENTS

�֍

3

✡

The story we live out isn't the story others read in the facts of our lives. The hardest autobiography to make is one that represents the flowing along of life felt from the inside out. But readers hear the tune they want to hear, not the one being played. I gag on the version strangers construct to explain my life—inner-city working-class person makes good: "How did someone like *you* become someone like *you*?" as someone actually once asked me—because it's pimped off American-style exceptionalism, which rots whatever it touches and saturates claims made for poetry and other art forms. It dances its bouncy polka with boosterism, another wasting disease smiling forth as peaches-and-cream health. Their compound poisons every culture—political, artistic, personal. Why should we need a National Poetry Month, that merry annual act of cultural contrition, unless we had a deep, souring anxiety about poetry's survival in a (historically formed) anti-intellectual culture? Boosterism serves up the Whitney Biennial and its striptease of competing voguish infantilisms. Video artist and easel painter alike have to be hot type, trailing money. Poets who comment on their art (or other arts, for that matter) tend to play screech trumpet to a crowd they think loves Maynard Ferguson, not Freddie Hubbard.

We get the culture we deserve and wish for. One screech screeches: Can poetry matter? Why should that even be a question? It matters if it's casually subversive and alters consciousness without being righteous. It doesn't matter much to me if poetry doesn't matter too much in the great world out there, even though I speak in these essays about my work as a poet. Poetry finds its way, sometimes on the sly, and insinuates its powers into our lives: it possesses what D. H. Lawrence calls "the insidious mastery of song." I also talk about movies, food and drink, cities, politics, music, and other matters. What counts is that the subjects are woven in a certain way into a certain life. Poetry, anyway, like other offerings, is contaminated by the huffy, celebrity-driven ethics of commerce, of peddling and consuming. All systems are the same system. Rumor forges fame, consumers have to be instructed (and really do want to know) what to pay attention to, and so reputations are made, desires shaped and fueled. The great nineteenth-century Italian poet Giacomo Leopardi says somewhere that the sure way to become famous is to have friends tell everyone they meet that you're already famous. I take it on faith that readers interested in the interfusings of life and culture, who believe that poetry brings what we need to know, brings questions we need to ask or conflicts we can't resolve, and who are patient with complexity—such readers don't have to be huckstered or harvested.

And yet for all my carry-on about exceptionalism and boosterism, here I am shrink-wrapping a version—fragmentary, selective, episodic, pontifical—of myself, a version I obviously prefer. My sense of things is that I was given, by my origins and the hard-angled circumstances that poke into anyone's life, a set of facts to live into, but the rest is a fairly vague, cranky story of aspiration and coming-into-consciousness. I don't desire scholarly distinction (I'm a lazy scholar anyway), but I do want a feeling for what it's like to make sense of what's given. My purpose in writing prose has been to communicate what it *feels* like to have thoughts, to look at images, to worry over words and their truths. An essay is life's fluidity momentarily shaped into a provisional, free-standing solid. To write essays is to respond to life with life, to counter-pressure reality's press. In a way, it's always ad hoc or on the wing, because the inner life keeps changing, troping along with whatever reality gives it to work with. The writer I've read most often, with belief in the truth of what he says, is William James, especially the truth of feeling for "the strungalong and flowing" sort of life we actually live.

And so I've chosen and sequenced these pieces to suggest a sensation of that strungalongness. The experiential fact-life I report here—the personalities, cities, streets, movie houses, dance halls, relationships—swims along and stirs with what my occasional interlocutors refer to as "the higher things" I've written about and looked at. There's no hierarchy. How could there be? My recitations, like most of their subjects, are unstable, they're not medallions of experience. My "background," the language of poetry I've practiced (shaped in part by that background), my criticism of artists and writers I've felt the need to talk back to—count among them Sid Caesar, David "Fathead" Newman, Diane Arbus, Marlon Brando, and Mario Lanza—everything streaks into everything else. That's the feeling I've tried to lay down here.

The essays are mostly new, with a few ringers from out-of-print collections (noted in the acknowledgments) that I've jimmied and remodeled to fit the book's shape. A few are squared-off critical essays on individual painters I've managed to *get* in recent years. The writing—all my writing—has been driven by awkward curiosity and uncertainty, a panicked desire for sights and sounds and sensations. So the story essayed here, such as it is, lurches and swerves. We often treat the things of fabricated culture—music, books, movies, pictures—as objects apart that a life observes, ponders, absorbs, and acquires for admiration, delight, pleasure. But finally the material here is inseparable from the porous membrane where facts drain into moments of intense, dizzied illumination. In *my* version, I haven't "arrived" anywhere: I'm still trying to find things, as I've been trying all along, and it's still a tumbling, pitched-forward action, pain spiked with pleasure, anxious ambiguity with wobbly, fugitive conclusions.

CITY DOG

1

FATHEAD'S HARD TIMES

When I'm standing at the opera—at ten dollars a ticket it's the best cheap show in San Francisco—I look along the balustrade and think on the kinds and degrees of backache that people will tolerate in exchange for a certain order of beauty. Regulars have to think things through in advance. The difference between the one-act *Salome*, a quick hundred minutes of sexed-up hysterics, and the nearly five-hour evening of the bitterly sweet *Così Fan Tutte* may entail significant medication. About opera I am the complete amateur, musically untrained, patchily familiar with the repertoire, but a concentrated listener and, like other hounds attracted by ripe scents, a helpless softie. Mostly I roll in it. Nothing else in my life induces the dark elation I feel at a performance of *Don Giovanni* or *Così*. Passages in *Rigoletto, Peter Grimes*, and *Jenufa* melt me down; and while I'm losing my mind during *Butterfly* I give no thought to Ezra Pound's crack in the *Cantos:* "Spewcini the all too human / beloved in the eyetalian peninsula / for quite explicable reasons."

I didn't grow up in the eyetalian peninsula, I grew up (in the 1950s and 1960s) in South Philadelphia, an operatic culture that gave no thought to opera. My neighborhood was working class, Italian Americans mostly, small congested squared-off redbrick row houses with shared stoops and walls, here and there a heroic sycamore, big voices aroused night and day, women's voices usually, shrieking at their disheveled ungrateful kids or at husbands coming home from miserable jobs. In the late 1950s through the 1960s, music of other sorts washed over every street and corner. They were the days of Berry Gordy's Motown Records and the sassy, big-finned-car vocals of Martha and the Vandellas, whose "Heat Wave" was an anthem to gluey city summers and sex. Phil Spector was crafting his "wall of sound" dynamics for The Ronettes, one of the early tough-girl groups, all beehive hairdos and Egyptian eye shadow. ("Be My Baby" still kills.) One of Spector's groups, The Teddy Bears, performed their hit "To Know Him Is to Love Him" on the TV dance show *American Bandstand*, broadcast from Philadelphia, which soon had its own city sound in The Delfonics (featured in Quentin Tarantino's *Jackie Brown*), two of whose singers were born the same year I was, 1945.

I listened with sunny transport to doo-wop groups. The Delfonics and The Deftones. The Clovers and The Cadillacs. The names alone would entice any daydreaming misfit to become some sort of writer. Transistors fizzed their portable sounds around the clock, indoors and out. On August nights men slept in deck chairs on the sidewalk, radios tuned to top ten programs ("We're livin' in a heat wave / a pain in your heart"), which in those days still featured vocals by Tony Bennett, Della Reese, and Sinatra. On summer weekends certain guys (bad guys taking a break from badness) did pretty much what you see in movies, cluster and croon on corners, leaning into the central harmonies they made. I sang a little myself, a passable falsetto, though I didn't go off with them later to make trouble at the local dance. Our basso profundo occasionally brought along a shot-putter's shot, which he once laid against the head of a black kid, a dark-complexioned, kinky-haired boy who danced with a white girl but who, the shot-putter later learned, was Sicilian.

My experience of music took a hard-angled and inauspicious turn when as a young boy I entered Pat's parlor, with its deeply folded odors of tomato sauce, cabbage, and garlic, down the block from the house I grew up in. Pat played mandolin and violin, it was said, though nobody had actually ever heard him play. My parents, who didn't care much about music of any kind, didn't know what to do with me. A multidisc 45 set of Sigmund Romberg's operetta *The Student Prince* had mysteriously turned up in our house. My father, who as staff handyman at a hospital had occasional access to useless pilfered goods like test tubes and fat rolls of butcher paper, might have acquired it after hearing me howl in the shower whatever stuck in my head from AM radio. (For weeks it was Jerry Lewis's nasal "Rockabye My

Baby.") Or it may have been the remnant of opera sets that some unknown immigrant uncle two generations back had owned. His collection, on acetate 78s, which in those days ran to twelve or more disks and weighed at least as much as a meat-slicer, had all been given to the Salvation Army when he died, or moved away, or disappeared. (Nobody could tell me what became of him.) "For Chrissake," my mother would say years later, "if I knew you'd end up liking that stuff, I'd've kept them." For weeks I played *The Student Prince* and sang along with Mario Lanza (Alfredo Arnold Cocozza adopted his mother's name, Maria Lanza), a South Philly boy from Mercy Street, where he and my uncle Mike played stickball, lustily shredding my voice just as he was shredding his. Shredding, too, the already threadbare fabric of family peace. And so I was sent to Pat, as some parents send their children to Boy Scout camp or a matinee.

I didn't expect so much silence. Pat spoke little English and taught me by the Italian method that had formed him. His parlor was like others in the neighborhood, with overcast weather and low clouds due to a high-pressure system—thickly upholstered, hard-spring furniture, statuettes of the Sacred Heart and Infant of Prague, and leaky table lamps. I was terrified. I didn't know what to expect, but vaguely thought I'd soon hold an instrument. Instead, to learn tempo, I clapped, for weeks. Clapped then waved my hand, side to side, as if in benediction of a privileged moment which never arrived, because along with the clapping Pat tried to teach me to read music. He wrote down and told me to copy notes and phrases that to me meant nothing, because they weren't voiced or sounded. Each week he *showed* me music and then sent me home to study it, clapping. I lived in a constant state of anxious boredom, stupefied by abstraction, and as unwilling to master unvoiced notes on the stave as I was to memorize the Latin that would have cleared me to become an altar boy. I felt so alive when my puny voice swelled alongside Mario's light tenor. But music, while I was learning it, became not just de-physicalized—it's made of nothing, after all—but abstract, virtual, a metronomic code embodied only by that robotic clapping and waving.

Weeks passed and I still hadn't seen an instrument. The idea was to start with mandolin and then work up to violin. What did I know? One day Pat drifted off like a poltergeist and returned with a mandolin, which he played a bit and let me touch but not hold. Next week, out came the violin. Same routine. He held out the instrument so that I could stroke it with my hand as if it was his pet, but infinitely remote, an actuality (it seemed an extension of his body) sealed off in a medium of mere possibility. I was Tantalus in the Parlor. Tantalized all the more when he tickled the mandolin into sound, then coddled and stroked long sonorous lines from the fiddle. Why wasn't I ecstatic? What I had known as a physically enthralling medium that came straight onto my nerves in mysterious, scary ways was becoming Idea. Luckily, that part of my musical education didn't last long. When I was eighteen and finally experienced live performance other than the snare drums and wheezing clarinets of wedding combos, it was at the Academy of Music during Eugene Ormandy's long stewardship of the Philadelphia Orchestra. Ormandy's predecessor Leopold Stokowski had created the plush, deep sonorities that came to be known as the "Philadelphia sound," as specific and laudatory a designation in the classical world as The Delfonics' sound was in theirs. I couldn't get enough. In the mid-1960s the orchestra performed a lot of Bartók and Mahler—I remember feeling that I was listening to the *Concerto for Orchestra* with my *stomach*—and I started paying attention to whatever was available on radio and the occasional LP I could afford. But my musical intake was what it still is, eclectic, a polite term for an indiscriminate slutty mess that took in Sunday morning gospel broadcast live from local Baptist churches, early Beatles and Stones, and jazz of any kind. In the end, probably because I always had rock and roll, *Bandstand,* and Mario singing "Golden Days" to fall back on, my interlude with Pat, instead of putting me off music or decisively cooling it into abstraction, jacked up music's nervous immediacy and made it even more systemic, brute, and ardent.

That physicality intensified when I was twenty years old and got sick, when music fused to physical pain. I've been in bondage, more or less, ever since, but it's a bondage—or bonding, a cellular hybridizing—I can't imagine living without. And it's formed by music of all sorts, especially, in my later life, by voice—Dawn Upshaw singing Marc Blitzstein, any good tenor's "Un Aura Amorosa" from *Così,* Sarah Vaughan accompanied by Clifford Brown, Dion's "The Wanderer," or Sting's a cappella "Roxanne" (which a dog I once knew, a Shih Tzu, sang along to with sonorous conviction). Physical pain is like personality: it's involuntarily expressive and idiosyncratic, but expressive only to the person experiencing it, and so idiosyncratic that any verbal representation of it is sickly inadequate and, to listeners especially, tedious, though talking about pain is boring first and most of all to its owner. It's an idiolect, a language specific to one brain and comprehensible only to the nervous system that activates and networks messages from that brain. It's grotesquely companionable to the person experiencing it but unfriendly toward others. It islands and isolates. When Philoctetes, in Euripides' play, dragging around his evil-smelling wounded foot, describes his island to the visiting Neoptolemus, he's also describing the exile that pain causes:

> There's no anchorage here, nowhere anyone
> can land or trade or have a good time.
> No sensible person sails this way,
> though now and then sailors come by,
> and when they do, they pity me,
> at least they say they do, and in their pity
> give me scraps of food and cast-off clothes.

Pain becomes you, becomes so capillary that even though it's local it colonizes the entire body and is coextensive with it. It saturates perceptions and your sense of consequence. While it's active, just as we say certain pieces of music irrationally change our lives, it can permanently alter your sense of sense.

Ankylosing spondylitis is a severe inflammation that breaks down ligaments and cartilage and fuses them to bone. If it's in the vertebrae, you end up with "bamboo spine." If the lower back, the sacroiliac joints become an inelastic boney mass. In 1965 the syndrome was unknown, so the pain that put me in the hospital for three months, then plateaued for ten years (a steep plateau, it was), and has faithfully stood by me in varying degrees—depending sometime on the length of the opera or band set—ever since, had no evident cause. The physical pain was fraught with the spiritual dread that unknowingness creates. I was tested for slipped disc, neurological damage, and psychosomatic dysfunction (i.e., derangement). Because the pain wasn't identifiable, my body felt invaded, colonized, by hostile unreason. A person my age whose A.S. went untreated now usually looks like a broken matchstick or twig, someone who, as a chiropractor friend of mine says, walks around looking at his shoes. (Imagine Groucho's scampish glide turned herky-jerky, Mr. Hyde-ish.) I've often seen old men in Chinatown shaped like grasshoppers, bent over a cane, looking up through inverted bifocals. Now I know why they look like that. My A.S. wasn't diagnosed until 2000, when a rheumatologist I consulted for a different ailment took an interest in my medical history and solved the mystery. He was rather surprised to see me standing upright. I *don't* walk around looking at my shoes, and for this I'm grateful to, among others, David "Fathead" Newman.

While in the hospital and for a long time thereafter, at night I kept by my ear a transistor radio like those the men who slept on sidewalks listened to. So whenever pain spiked me awake—*it* seemed deranged, because it migrated: now in my lower back, now knees, now upper legs—I had sounds running into my ear that instead of being a balm or distraction layered me more deeply into the pain, its rhythms and registers. The pain and its music, as one entity, took on the sort of casual familiarity Nietzsche describes in *The Gay Science:* "I have given a name to my pain and call it 'dog.' It is just as faithful, just as obtrusive and shameless, just as entertaining, just as clever as any other dog—and I can scold it and vent my bad mood on it."

My night music was jazz, spun by Joel Dorn at Philadelphia's FM station, WHAT, which programmed around the clock. Early Nina Simone, Oliver Nelson's *The Blues and the Abstract Truth,* Miles Davis playing Gil Evans's arrangements, Oscar Peterson's sweet and melancholy *Canadian Suite,* and the celestial Charles Lloyd. Dorn, who went on to become an astute, adventurous record producer, hosted an evening radio show to which he brought some interesting backstory. In 1958, as a teenager already possessed by blues and jazz, Dorn went to a small joint outside Philadelphia called the Ambler Sporting Club, where Ray Charles and his group were performing. Charles was mostly a rhythm and blues instrumentalist starting to break ground as a pop vocalist and jazz artist. The sax player in Charles's ensemble was a young and handsome fellow named David "Fathead" Newman. (When he flubbed an arpeggio in his high school band, the leader called him a fathead, and the moniker stuck.) Dorn cornered him during a break between sets and promised him that someday, when he became a DJ, he would use a number he heard that night, "Hard Times," as his theme song.

And so he did, every night at 10 P.M. All day every day I felt the urge to take to bed and settle into whatever occult infirmity waited there for me. I didn't know, of course, that if I did so, my body would shape itself to its illness, and once I put on my shoes I would spend a long time looking at them. We now know that certain rheumatic disorders require the body to stay in motion lest it stiffen for good. Some impulse, maybe fear of inertia— I became terrified, still am, by enforced immobility—or mule-headedness, made me want to stay in motion. With the help of stout canes given me by my Mario-Lanza Uncle Mike, who lost a leg in the war, I rode the bus into center city, went up and down subway stairs and the stairs in our small dim house (occasionally harangued by my impossible mother about how much suffering I was causing her), and walked endless circles—ovals, actually—around the dining room table, to train my legs again, to walk the dog. Keep moving, I told myself, like jazz, which is most alive in its changes.

By late evening the pain was running high; I'd be exhausted and have to rest. "Hard Times," Ray Charles on piano opening with a brief, tripping statement of theme, was always waiting for me. Fathead's sax line, a climbing plea resisting the drag of melancholy, became a resting place for (not from) pain, became pain's reliable nocturnal climate and substance. I loved the number all the more, with the kind of exasperated love that doesn't fade but gets more acute in memory, even after the pain dampened. I never owned the album, though, until recently, when I ran down a remastered CD of the original 1958 LP, *Fathead: Ray Charles Presents David Newman*. "Hard Times" is the opening track, and when I played it, not having heard it for over thirty years, I wept like a child for the past, and then I whistled along.

In the hospital, I had nothing but time on my hands and pain in my brain. I spent time practicing apotropaic mind games I hoped would help with the pain. What they now call "pain management" is really a way of establishing terms of ownership. One tactic is to contrive likenesses. Pain is a language, a story, a journey, it's a busted gearbox's teeth, a bed of nails, a heat gun. Another, and one I practiced for years, is to imagine the means of eliminating it. Extirpating it. I imagined marking its boundaries, as one traces the frontiers of a small country on a map, then surgically knifing it out, carving it clear of its surrounding mass of nerve and flesh as Filipino hoodoo men magically insert their hands into a sick person and extract the ailing part. I could, I thought, use a trowel or ice-cream scoop or child's sand shovel and remove it cleanly. I wouldn't want to see it or dedicate it to science. I wanted an old high school pal, a racketeer trainee, to take it away and feed the gorgeously veined, placental mass to the rats and feral cats at the dump.

My reading kept pain company. I read Thomas Mann's *Doctor Faustus*, his "Nietzsche book" about the inseparability of sublimity and pain. Adrian Leverkühn, a prodigious young composer and inventor of tone-row music, in order to break through ("like a butterfly emerging from its chrysalis") to an original musical language for feeling, to something really new—it turns out to be plainsong—sells his soul to the devil by contracting the syphilis that kills him and bargaining away love. Immobilized, often in hip-harness traction ("counter-indicated," they would now say), I moved laboriously through Mann's high-toned, immobile prose. What else was there to do? Except in the movies and TV, hospitals are generally uneventful places, the sick waiting to learn more about sickness, lose it, or succumb. So I was cheered by the occasional visits of an African American orderly who would stop by on his rounds to chat with the poor young bastard in bed. Actually, I was cheered before he walked in. I knew he was approaching because he'd be whistling, pitch-perfect, some jazz standard, and so in addition to the emotional boost he brought, he reminded me of a character in *Doctor Faustus*, the violinist Rudolph Schwerdtfeger, who "whistled with such artistry that one laughed for sheer pleasure, whistled more like a violin than a flute, the phrasing masterly, the little notes, staccato or legato, coming out with delirious precision."

The eeriest jazz stylist then (featured of course on WHAT) was Morgana King. After cutting a few albums and attracting a small but devoted following, she shunted into an acting career, so that most people now know her only as Don Corleone's stolid wife in the *Godfather* movies. Her repertoire was jazz classics and pop ballads like "A Taste of Honey," the title of her first LP. Some singers emulate the solidified sound of string instruments. King's voice went the opposite way. Her delivery was wound tight, breathy, flute-ish, air tremulously whisked into resonance, closer to moody, throaty whistling than to song. Her singing reminded me of the orderly's whistling. That was a time when you still heard people whistling everywhere, in hospital corridors and buses, in workplaces and on the street. I once read a lament by some poet about the passing of those sounds from public and private life. But they haven't entirely passed. The day I was reading the lament I could hear my adolescent daughter about the house whistling some Chopin she was working up on piano; that reedy vitality gave me a rush of affection and hope, for her and for all breath in life, but rattled me, too, because it made me think of breath passing, my own, hers. And a childhood South Philly friend was visiting at the time, who in the many years I've known him whistles phrases the way people whoop at ball games and concerts, violent gusts and surging wing-beats of sound, but always only a phrase or two, which seems to exhaust him, because he never completes a melodic line. It's true enough that outdoors—I have no car, so I spend a lot of time waiting for and riding public transit—I hardly ever hear anybody whistling, and I don't have to catch myself if I start doing so because heads immediately turn my way, as if I'd burst into song. But who can say that's a bad thing? There's not much whistling going on because so many people are listening to music, ears muffed or buttoned up by headsets.

I tried another tactic while I was laid up, whistling through (or along with) the pain while the music was playing. Pain breathes forth its rhythms and tonalities through its instrument, the body. If I breathed too deeply, cleared my throat, or, God help me, coughed, pain spiked. Once I sneezed and nearly passed out. ("Give that boy more Darvon and muscle relaxers!") When people around me whistle, I listen up, thinking I'll hear some essence revealed, because it's breath. I sat vigil with my mother until she stopped breathing. Before he died my father's breath thinned to a hesitant narcotized hum. An old neighborhood friend of mine recently died in his sleep. Our lunch dates every couple of months were a ritual, the sort of little social celebration that refreshes and sustains affection: we ate at the same time in the same neighborhood place, even ate the same dishes—I did, anyway; he flopped between two favorites. Inside the restaurant, when I sat or stood, the standard but by now dampened pain flicked its blowtorch, as it likes to do. (My darling remembers me.) But I was happy when we settled down to catch up, gossip, talk books and movies and mutual friends, then say goodbye with a peck on the cheek, until next time. He loved to eat and drink and get lost. One night after dinner at my apartment, I was playing Dion and the Belmonts, and when he stood to leave he starting juking and pumping his fists to "The Wanderer"—"I'm a wanderer / Yes, a wanderer / I go around around around around"—right there in my kitchen. Whenever I phoned to make a lunch date, while fumbling for his book he whistled in a way that bespoke his personality, a bit diffident, unobtrusive, more air than tone, and no tune really, just a happy-go-lucky breathy jaunt. Now I wait for a streetcar on our neighborhood corner where I sometimes ran into him, hearing no whistling at all, and I feel as if he disappeared into his own breath, the small music he made, and took all that beautiful rough vitality with him.

GOTS IS WHAT YOU GOT

What are beginnings? A constantly melting and recomposing amalgam of images? A sentence we keep writing and revising? A messy album in which we seek patterns to explain to ourselves the mystery of personality? One of my favorite passages in John Ruskin's autobiography, *Praeterita*, describes the soft orchestration of his family's voices:

> I never had heard my father's or mother's voice once raised in any
> question with each other, nor seen an angry, or even a slightly hurt
> or offended, glance in the eyes of either. I had never heard a servant
> scolded, nor even suddenly, passionately, or in any severe manner,
> blamed.

His household must have been a walled garden of mild manners. This is a powerful legend of childhood to me because it's so grotesquely remote from my own, which was charged with the electricity of blame, of real or presumed or anticipated offense. There were few mild manners in my family or the immigrant neighborhood where I grew up. Mildness was a liability. In a boy it attracted predators like a scent. You were wrong to choose mildness as a way of meeting the world, because it was a flaw in the stone of personality, a symptom of sickness. A diffident, soft-spoken man like my father (who had breakdowns just like a friend of his, the only other mild-mannered man I remember from our circle of friends) was considered weak, inadequate, disabled in spirit, though the nicety people used to conceal this conviction was to say he was (like his shattered friend) "a good man."

The voices of my world were not tender and unquestioning. Conversations, especially among members of my mother's family, were choleric eruptions. If by some accident a rational argument occurred, defeat was registered not by words of acknowledgment but by a sardonic, defiant sneer. (We were masters of the mannered condescension Pope describes in his "Epistle to Doctor Arbuthnot": "And without sneering, teach the rest to sneer.") Anger, impatience, and dismissive ridicule of the unfamiliar were the most familiar moods. Everyone around me, it seemed, except for my father's side of the family, spoke in the brittle, pugnacious tones I still hear when my own voice comes snarling out of its vinegary corner. My neighbors, having no servants to scold, scolded one another. There were no degrees of criticism or disapproval, only a single absolute pitch of dismissal. I heard it from when I was a child until I was an adolescent, when my friend Joey T., a sweet-hearted boy who sat behind me in homeroom, eagerly offered to shoot a teacher (a Norbertine priest) who was tormenting me. A year earlier, he wanted to do the same to a kid who was bullying me: "I'll shoot the son of a bitch in the face!" Later, after I'd left South Philadelphia, I encountered different sorts of polite, well-bred nastiness and intolerance practiced by other sorts of people, casually genteel Protestant expressions of "displeasure" that made me nostalgic for the operatic candor of my own culture.

A disruptive megaphone tonality was also the medium for affection or delight, the way a shriek can indicate terror or frivolity. It wasn't, in any case, an excitability people directed at one another. I hardly ever heard anyone in my family or neighborhood say they were angry with (or fond of) so-and-so. It was instead an aimless but earnest wrathfulness or rapture, theatrical and purposeless, a kind of roving sparkiness going off constantly in the universe at large, for it took in God and all His angels and His saints. My people always seemed to be picking a fight with circumstance, with the very *fact* of circumstance, and in the absence of specific aggravating circumstance the cosmos would do. I didn't know how peculiar this was until I left it behind and found outside my culture a broader and more pliable medium for moral feeling. Nor did I realize how deeply its music had settled in my heart until I heard in the poetry I came to write that same extremity of unease and rage at circumstance.

The two sides of my family were the hemispheres of my temperament. My mother's family, which set the dominant tone in our lives, came from a village near Naples whose name no one remembers, though my eldest aunt was born there and my grandparents, Carmela and Simone, lived there until their twenties. The Girone clan had the classic Neapolitan temperament, a volatile compound of hilarity, raucous grief, anger, and consternation over every one of life's details—a culture of sublime complaint, of rage or hysteria in the presence of divinely sponsored fate. Grandfather Simone, after emigrating to Philadelphia, worked off and on as a rough carpenter, drinking too much off and on and often drunkenly whipping his children with a belt strap, as he later menaced us grandchildren. His longest on-the-job stint was underground, working along with hundreds of immigrant laborers to build the Philadelphia subway system. His wife died after giving birth to their sixth child. My mother, the third of four daughters, became responsible for the family, and when she married my father, she brought Grandfather Simone along. He lived with us for many years, and when he died at ninety-three, gruffly attributing his age to robust bloodlines, dago red, and blackleaf stogies, he spoke maybe fifty words of English, most of them obscenities that sparked from his mouth whenever Eliot Ness and his archangels killed Italian gangsters on *The Untouchables*, Italian gangsters played by Greeks, black Irish, and Jews. One night, drunk and in uncharacteristic jolly spirits, he confided to me that in Italy he had once killed a man over an insult and did jail time. I never determined the truth of this. None of his children would confirm or deny it. "Oh," they said, "Pop says all sorts of crazy things."

The Di Piero side seemed a different country. In a sense it *was* a different country, given the distinct identities of Italy's regions. The emotional and intellectual climate of the Di Piero hemisphere was so different that even now, thinking it, I feel it. The Neapolitan Girones were voluble, brash, impetuous, defiant, and proud of their toughness. The Abruzzese Di Pieros were reserved, quiet-spoken, self-contained, and they reflected more complexly on the particulars of experience. The Girones felt that too much thinking would make you crazy, complexity was a kind of sinfulness, so I was in bad water from the start. Among the Girones I felt I was being watched, among the Di Pieros I was being seen. My father, his younger brother, and sister took after their mother, Maria, all gentle, reticent souls. I've visited the small hilltop town in Abruzzo called Castel Frentano where my father was born. The people of Abruzzo, they say, are *fort'e gentili*, strong and kind. Regional traits shouldn't fit so snugly as that one fits the Di Pieros. Their laughter was different, small and almost diffident, less assaultive than Girone laughter. Different memory hoards, too. Both families were poor but managed to make decent lives in the New World after much hard work. Grandmother Maria, however, kept a store of knowledge about the old country, the crossing in steerage, her husband Aurelio who died just a few years after arriving in America, her own situation as a young widow speaking no English, three children to support, the years in a sweatshop, and all the rest. It was she who told me, sometimes only vaguely, of our ancestors: the priest who left his property to the prostitute who had given birth to his child, the Di Pieros who left for South America and started new families there without dissolving their first ones in Italy, the collateral masses of Di Pieros in Argentina and Brazil descendant from those ancestors—gamblers, settlers, plantation tycoons.

The Girones were another immigrant mentality: they knew nothing about their past and preferred it that way. Grandfather Simone was the only one who could tell us anything, but the only story he told me was the one about the killing. For the Girones the New World was a happy oblivion. For the Di Pieros there remained some sense of the gleaming shadows of past lives. Even their way with language was worlds apart. Maria spoke real Italian, though with occasional dialect words, the swallowed vowel-endings of immigrant speech, and the southernish accent of Abruzzo. Simone spoke only dialect, which isn't conventional language spoken with eccentric vocabulary and syntax; it's a different language. A Bolognese visiting Naples can hardly understand a conversation in Neapolitan. When, in my twenties, I finally learned Italian, I conversed happily with my grandmother and, when she was dying, wrote letters for her in Italian to her relatives in Abruzzo. When my grandfather was dying, we tried to communicate, but his dialect was as unintelligible to me as my standard Italian was to him.

In my house, the Girone temper dominated, so relations were tense, disputatious, eroded by suspicion, resentment, and spleen. The sense of the world those voices communicated to me was that contingency, the fact of living in the world only to die, *disputed* human presence. The most of bird life that I saw in South Philadelphia were starlings, grackles, pigeons, and sparrows hopping around sewer grates. Later on I began to love to watch the varieties of birds—the body sustained in a medium of apparent nothingness, at home there. Canada geese barking one fall morning in Vermont. A cardinal flashing in a snowy wood. A cuckoo calling outside a farmhouse in Calabria. Dawn's starling screech in South Philadelphia. The lesson I absorbed from the rough vocal music of my childhood was that we cannot be entirely at home in the world because we have a consciousness that dreams of elsewheres—heavens and whatnot. Tenants, not stewards, of the world, and the world behaves like a miserly indifferent landlord.

From when I was very young I was attracted, by the call of what is sensually and intellectually elsewhere, to what Yeats called "sweet sounds together." When I began to read poetry, sheer tonal musicality was more important than subject matter. I read whatever I happened upon in the public library. Poe, Lindsay, Millay, Sandburg, the Byron of "The Prisoner of Chillon," some anthology pieces by Wordsworth and Whitman. Bits out of Homer and the Arthurian tales absorbed me mostly with the velocity of narrative, the tidal progress of surge and arrest, and the pitch of the telling. In good time, I became aware of tonality as event and felt my way into the formal pliability of language. Whatever is authentic in my work is due to the crass commingling of that abstract sense of formal beauty with the given language textures and soul-conditions of my culture, though when I was struggling for postadolescent intellectual and cultural independence, I of course believed I had to refine out the "crudities" of my culture. And yet I never did shed my tribal legacy of contrariness, the festive abrasiveness and chafing hilarity that even now I still at once love and cringe at. It took me some time to realize that abrasiveness, mineral grit, could be the kind of pumice stone that polishes a surface and gives shapely forms a chased gleam.

Sour exasperation, shrill gaiety, raspingly curt affection, these were the registers most familiar to me. In my childhood, the words themselves were often not even English. I once walked into our corner grocery operated by a noble, solemn Calabrese named Gumbo. (Who knows what Italian nickname that comic English sound violated?) It was a Friday in Lent, *baccalá* was soaking in a basin outside, I was the only customer, and Gumbo and his wife were arguing furiously. The wife grabbed a can from a shelf and threatened to throw it at Gumbo's head. Though I could understand bits of my grandparents' different languages, I understood nothing of what Gumbo and his wife were shouting. When I reported this to my mother—I was seven, I sneaked from the store without interrupting the quarrel, shaking with fear not only of the savage feelings displayed but of all that fiercely directed unintelligibility—she explained how Gumbo and his wife weren't a good match and didn't get along in the first place, and second, they spoke different dialects and couldn't understand each other. He was Calabrese, she was from Aldilá. When I asked where Aldilá was, she said somewhere up north. "Who the hell knows? *Up there.*" Aldilá, so far as I know, is no place-name. Or only in a special sense. The prepositional phrase *al di lá* means "beyond." (*Al di lá del fume* = the other side of the river.) In Dante, it means the beyond, heaven, a beatific elsewhere. Where, then, was Gumbo's wife from? "Aldilá!" my mother and her sisters shrieked at me, as if to increase my understanding, pointing north.

North of where? Naples? South Philadelphia (for us the center of the known world)? Who the hell knows? I knew Gumbo and his family well. He was a great lover of horticulture in that row house neighborhood without plants and flowers. He once took me to Bartram's Garden, a patch of land planted with native and exotic flora in the eighteenth century by the Quaker farmer John Bartram, where I nearly passed out from the powerful fragrances. He spoke halting English. When he quarreled with his wife, who spoke fluent English, they quarreled in their dialects. (Language as warring nation-states.) In those intensest moments, they became foreigners to each other. To communicate grievance and ferocity they relied entirely on tone, gesture (that can of tomato paste!), and pitch. For most of the people I was raised among, it was ferocity, real or theatrical, that mattered; defiant energy was our way of meeting the world and pretending we weren't subject to its harsh ministrations and unfair judgments. Sense, reason, logic, sequence, sounds strung together intelligibly or coherently or sweetly or gently— these were suspect, untrustworthy, often signs of the power that other forces (bureaucracies, governments, professional agencies, outsiders) exercised to the harm or humiliation of people like us.

In *Praeterita* Ruskin describes himself as a boy: "I already disliked growing older—never expected to be wiser, and formed no more plans for the future than a little black silkworm does in the middle of its first mulberry leaf." In time, we lose the silkworm's constant appetitive present. Expectations grow in us the way language inflects itself into more complex verb tenses, and they become the fungus that corrodes the leaf. One of my soul's conditional tenses ("if only . . .") has always been to live the silkworm's moment, completely in the instant, but even to *think* that is an act of migratory mind, of the imagination making images of elsewheres. The Northumbrian poet Basil Bunting writes in his great poem, *Briggflatts*, that the poet "lies with one to long for another." The present tense is the stolid, dispassionate judge and minister to the encroachments of the tempter, the "if only" or "what if" or "were it so." I've never felt alarmed by an issue we've heard much about in recent years—the "marginality" of poetry in American culture. It's usually tied to traditional powers which poetry has presumably surrendered to other arts. I believe poetry can still express, more completely and with more complexity than other media, feeling in time and feeling for time. Verb tenses mix, coalesce, bang, and sag. The senses reckoning with their local reality, the heart reckoning with the political relations noded therein and radiating therefrom—poetry makes these a right, fit matter of speech. If we turn these energies into mere issues or "crises" we're conceding their incipient powers. But this may also be an admission that poetry no longer wants or needs to give voice to the passion of consciousness. The issue is not whether poetry is adequate to the task (though the question figures in harmless after-dinner speeches at poetry banquets), but the ways in which it goes about executing the task. For me, it's not by means of genteel manners and overrefined sensibility but by using language as a constant viewing or scanning of origins, with ongoing recognitions of reality layered in. Not local-coloristic origins—local color cans a sentimentalized version of fact—but the beginnings of species consciousness as they figure forth in local conditions, local cultures. The migratory passion of imagination, of image-making, burns in the instant.

When I was growing up, my ear trained only a little on the sounds of words in books and mostly on the cadences and textures of language spoken around me. The idioms I heard, their racy patterns and fiery tonalities, were often only partly released from an Italian bedrock. Since nearly every adult and most of my playmates had spoken some sort of Italian, the English we heard and used was a strangely colored flower sprung from sandy soil. The Neapolitan dialect the Girones spoke sounded eruptive and jabby. English words with Italianate endings tumbled from unintelligible dialect phrases. *Boifrendo* for "boyfriend." *Baccaus* for "back house" or bathroom, because the privy was always back of the house. English phrases sometimes translated Italian idioms. Women in my family still say "I'll give you eat" because it translates *Ti do mangiare*. I heard a disapproving father threaten his postadolescent son, who was trying to raise a beard, with the hilariously ominous cry: "I'll break your face with that chin!" Italian sounds fused to English ones. English itself was a marshland of strange fogs and apparitions. Antsy, Esso, rumdumb, rock candy, coalbin. Tootsie pop sounded kin to tootsie brute, which was how people sounded out *Tu sei brutta* (too say BROOT-ah, pronounced instead as tootz ay BROOT), literally "You're ugly" but spoken as an endearment to children, like "Little funny face." The vulgarism *cazzo* (CAHTS-zo, "cock" or "prick," but used like "fuck," e.g., *Ma che cazzo fai* = What the fuck are you doing) was pronounced *gahtz*. I heard it said a hundred times: You got gots is what you got. You don't have a goddamn thing.

The English I was listening to in the 1950s—I remember it as listening, not hearing or overhearing—was one expression of the unstable, poorly bred vernacular which forty years earlier Henry James said would become the emergent language of the immigrant populations flooding American cities. It was a vitally impure, try-it-on language bearing the burrs and toothy surfaces of languages more or less left behind in Europe and western Russia, with regional dialects showing up as weird watermarks on those surfaces. The sentences I read in my schoolbooks were, by contrast to my neighborhood music, affectless and imperial. My feeling for idiomatic speech became studied, self-conscious. I feared the embarrassment of misspeaking an idiom or cracking a malapropism. I still have to pay attention when I use catchphrases, commonplaces, idiomatic turns of speech, for fear of getting them wrong. I still commit to memory and rehearse common turns of phrase I hear on the street. I became a poet who seeks conversational normalcy and vigor in poetry the way one seeks out a distant constellation. My instinct is the still childish one of taking what's given in language and breaking it up into phonetic pieces, syllable amulets, each loaded with some nuance of actual or desired feeling and the pied, scattered clues of sense. The cunning of Emily Dickinson's "Tell all the truth but tell it slant, / Success in circuit lies" is strategic. What happens when your *given* English is in many ways cockeyed or skewed and draws force and complexity from that? The artifice most difficult to sustain is, for me, that of casual normalcy. The amiable, knowing style of much contemporary poetry sounds to my ear as phony as the King's English. (It may in fact be, culturally and politically, the King's English of our time, official and self-assured, but that's a different question.)

Working the language of poetry has been for me a struggle to momentarily stabilize what is by nature and culture off, unstable, riddled with fabulous, obscene errors.

My South Philadelphia language could be brutal, and it was to my heart the purest expression of unreason, solemnity, and discontent. But it was also an impoverished instrument for clear reasoning or exact description; it lived in my mind as an enemy of such activities—impatient, stupidly superstitious, intolerant of rational deliberation, suspicious of coherences and consistencies. It blended into its tones and rhythms a sense of the sacred. But *sacre* means both sacred and accursed. We spoke of physical and psychological sickness as if it were the presence of a god among us. This was felt especially with regard to mental disorders, which were carefully separated from other sicknesses. The young bachelor on my block who was epileptic, the woman who moved objects with the power of her mind, the girl who possessed second sight—they were holy presences. But the friend of my father who had a nervous breakdown and wept helplessly for days at the kitchen table before being finally hospitalized was not sacred or possessed by the god. He was a pollution, shameful and scandalous—his disorder was like blood spilled in sanctified precincts. Neighborly expressions of sympathy were ritualized conventions of speech meant to contain the menace, seal off the pollution. The word "sickness" had an aura of mysterious visitation and violation. The phrase "nervous exhaustion" (*esaurimento nervoso*—I learned it in my twenties, long before I'd use it to describe my own experience) signaled some degree of moral expulsion from the community. They should have said, and I would have been better off to hear, that his soul was sick or damaged or fatigued. Physical illness was attributable to divine intent, it was some kind of election and was fingered by deity. Nervous trouble was a humiliation, not an affliction, because it was so entirely a human condition, or a sign of having been abandoned by the gods. When I began to find my way as a poet, I wanted to make poetry seem an awareness of the world lived along the nerves, but ministered to by the difficult clarities of reason and judgment. The blunt play and immediacy of my local language was given to me. I had to learn the rest.

LOVE FOR SALE

A few years ago in the Museum of Modern Art I was sitting on a bench before a prime Jackson Pollock from the late 1940s. I was doing my thing, that thing I do whether I'm reviewing an exhibition, preparing an essay, trying to find my way toward something as yet indistinct, or simply scoping random pleasures: I looked the picture over and then closed in on passages and concentrated with a world-detached attentiveness, in which state I (irrationally, while thinking it entirely normal) expect the object to respond to *me,* to fix itself in memory, to enter and change me. Then—for this too is part of the act of paying attention—my mind drifted and began to saw away at the trivia of daily life: appointments, fragments that might stream into a piece of writing, and what was the name of that person I met last night? And what were our exact parting words? Soon enough the dust motes blew away and I was aware again of being present before an image, getting webbed into its field of meaning, waiting for its reality to intensify. On the bench next to me sat a smiling man—who knows how long he'd been there?—dressed casually, but not in the khaki pants, virgin-snow running shoes, and knit pullover of your standard-issue out-of-towner. Sport coat, checked shirt, slacks; presentable, utterly nondescript. He didn't look like a professional anything. And yet he wore that lost, blissful smile. The weekend crowd poked and swiveled around us, most with ears suctioned to their Acoustiguides, no one giving the picture more than the cursory fifteen-second once-over occasionally goosed by an "O wow!" or "This I don't get."

In big-city museums and galleries, especially New York's, you never know what stranger will materialize beside you and commence an oration or critique. Once, at a show of Arshile Gorky's portraits, a woman with fizzy, gray, nuclear-cloud hair materialized just so, more or less mid-sentence, and went on about the supreme loving melancholy in Gorky's portrait of himself as a child with his mother, one of two that he made. The boy stands, tentative and anxious, downcast gaze nearly catatonic, listing toward the seated sad mother, holding a bunch of flowers. He looks as if he's trying to graft his body onto her strength. Both look as if they've just seen something awful. I mentioned to my newfound companion that the mother effectively starved herself to death during the diaspora of Armenians fleeing the Turkish genocide of 1916 so that little Arshile and his sister could survive and take ship for America. My acquaintance, a fine-looking person quivering with glamour and enthusiasm, asked more questions, so we went around and looked at a few more pictures together, then she pulled a Manhattan Mandrake and was gone. Just like that. I never even saw her leave the gallery. And yet, in that briefly improvised intimacy, we'd talked of loyalty, sacrifice, and love.

"They don't know what they're missing." This, in a proprietary wondering tone, from the man sharing my bench, who looked so immobilized, so *stilled*, that he might have been there for hours. His comment had no bite of disdain. It was the soft-shoe equivalent of a mad movie scientist jumping up and down cackling, "It's *mine*! All *mine*!" He was laying claim to the picture, taking possession of it emotionally and intellectually. It's worth possessing. *Number 1A, 1948* is one of Pollock's earliest drip paintings, an arterial system of wiry pigment looping and shooting end to end across a creamy yellow-white ground, with gaseous cerulean patches floated softly in the textures and tiny lipstick-red kisses puckering up through the layers. The face of the man beside me wore the pleasurably stupefied, mashed look of someone in love.

It happens to the best (and worst) of us. Love at first sight. Or passing infatuation that in the maturity of time turns to a love so complete and enthralling that it shapes our feeling for reality. Or young love, puppy love, hapless crushes, the loss of all sense to an object that gives nothing back. Or studious love: Tell me more about yourself, I'm patient as the summer day is long, and don't you think such-and-such is interesting? Cole Porter gave words to how we make ourselves available: "Love for sale. Who will buy? / Who would like to sample my supply? / Who's prepared to pay the price / For a trip to

Paradise?" We don't, can't really, love pictures the way we love others. Flesh is both object and medium of love. It has its unpredictable mutability and felt pulse. The Spanish philosopher Ortega y Gasset, a favorite of American intellectuals half a century ago but now seldom read, in his little 1957 book, *On Love*, says that desire, once fulfilled, disappears, but that love is forever unsatisfied. It's essentially an act of impassioned attention, and when it starts, when we fall hard, we're madly attentive. Shakespeare's lunatic and lover are of imagination all compact because they possess an aberrant, abnormal attention span. Like most experience that begins with a calamitous rush of feeling, love evens out in time and becomes normalized, sometimes (if we don't pay attention) dulled or killed by habit and familiarity.

Being in love is a condition, but love itself is all process. Ortega calls it "a psychic radiation which proceeds from the lover to the beloved, not a single discharge, but a current." Once we've fallen for a picture, we sustain our love by paying ongoing attention, revisiting it when possible, spending time in its company, sometimes via a print or postcard which, like the snapshot of a beloved, spills a stew of feelings, recollections, yearnings. When we've lived with a picture for a long time, we feel we're reciprocating an intimate attention *it* has given *us*. Wooing, love's preliminary, is the making and shaping of questions, of erotic inquiries to which we don't really expect answers just yet. (Postwooing, we expect the person or picture to provide us with something that sustains sensation and spirit.) We formulate questions in our heads. We talk to ourselves, or talk back, as I think that Pollock lover was doing: Why do that? How did Pollock get that far? Why am I feeling like this? Talking to oneself about a picture is yet another productively maniacal activity. What matters most is spiritual and intellectual motion, the rhythmic oscillation of words formed in our heads and radiated out to the object.

Sometimes the things of the world mediate our love of another. Storms, subway noise, a warm breeze, silverware alert in drawers, bedside lamp, linen, photograph or painting. One of the heaviest moments of flirtation in my life happened in the Museum of Modern Art in front of *Summation*, a big Gorky abstraction of sexy, biomorphic forms. The moment packed a charge because my woo-ee and I knew that anything we said about the picture would taste deliciously peppery. The Pollock man was, I'd guess, quietly experiencing his own sort of frenzy, a state of bliss he knew he could revisit. He was certainly traveling high and low, in the country of Plato's "Love is desire for generation and birth in beauty," and in crooning doo-wop land.

HATS

When Pat the number writer stopped by our house once a week, he went through a series of removals. He took off his brown felt fedora, took from its sweatband a square of folded foolscap, took from his pocket a golf pencil to write down the numbers my parents wanted to play, and then took their money. The one time my father hit on a nickel bet, Pat pulled from the sweatband a blackened five-dollar bill folded like a paper airplane. For me—I was seven or eight—he was all hat. Most men were, in the early 1950s. Construction workers in watch caps, white-collar workers in fedoras, the occasional baseball or golf cap. Exotic seasonal things like the summer boater and winter deerstalker worn by my next-door neighbor who sported jazz bows and a pencil mustache. My father wore a porkpie to the hospital where he did maintenance work. The one time I visited him, he was wearing, in sideways Rootie-Kazootie manner, a Dutch Boy painter's cap. On springtime Sundays before Mass, after fussing with his starched collar and Windsor knot, he put on a dressy gray straw snap-brim. Although the sign outside our local laundry, "Hats Cleaned and Blocked," meant nothing to me, I knew it was something I someday wanted to have done.

The women wore scarves, sometimes knotted around their necks like French apache dancers, topped off maybe with a beret, like Sharon Stone in *Sliver*. Or babushkas, which made them look mournfully just and just off the boat, true greenhorns, which some of them were. A few covered their toddlers' heads with babushkas, which made them look suspicious and wise.

In spring and summer women wrapped their heads in bandanas when they scrubbed front steps or butchered chickens in the backyard. Women elders like my grandmother made their long hair into prim empress bonnets.

The things neighborhood men and women wore on their heads gave them the slightly hooded look we children learned growing up, the kind you see in photos of immigrants. Hats were, still are, signage: "Don't Mess with Me." "Minding My Own Business." "Crazed and Unpredictable." As teenagers, headgear was our animal coloring—to repel, attract, or camouflage. We never walked straight on at black boys sporting doo-rags to protect their process. Now NBA players, unprocessed, sport them for street cred, as Latino gangbangers do. Kids now pull woolen caps down around their ears, covered with a sweatshirt hood, like medieval knights draping their heads with chain mail before putting on a helmet.

Hats were theatrical, too. Street vendors made them part of their schtick: the ragpicker wore a jaunty locomotive engineer's cap; the pretzel guy a Phillies cap turned backward. In the movies, black Stetsons were like catechism's blackened milk bottles signifying a soul drenched in mortal sin; only lean, sadistic men wore them, southerners usually, men you might expect to make children work like chattel. Sometimes the theatricality is harmless and happy. On Haight Street I see kids in period costumes outside a swing dance club, their wide-brims and flat tops performing before they do. The gutter punks, their thick knit caps harnessing dreadlocks, look on with bewildered disapproval.

In my daughter's favorite snapshot of me, taken many years ago, I'm wearing a beret and looking fierce, which I'm not, though I may have been then, a little. It's her favorite, I think, because it performs a personality, a spirit presence she wants or needs to make of me. And which may be true. I've made similar use of a photo of my father wearing that springtime snapbrim, where he looks happy as I never saw him to be in life. And one of my mother in a nightclub with a gardenia in her hair, a stunning brunette looking flirty, which she was, and gentle, which she wasn't.

Lewis Hine's photographs, which I've used as talismans of reality in my adult life, don't offer any kind of deliverance. His early twentieth-century pictures of child workers in South Carolina cotton mills or Baltimore canneries, of dark immigrants in dark bowlers, of barefoot-poor boys smoking fag ends, are completed historical facts. A textile mill foreman is fixed in our historical imaginations as the merciless overseer of the rickety, downy boys standing beside him. A ragpicker, too, is archived in one of Hine's photos, but the historical fact is that he's constantly in process of becoming the tattered sheaves he carries.

STENDHAL SYNDROME

On January 22, 1817, before he became "Stendhal," Henri Beyle—journalist, opera-going bon vivant, travel writer, biographer—descends the Apennines by coach toward Florence. He's charged up. "My heart was leaping wildly within me," he writes in his journal. "What utterly childish excitement!" We all feel such excitement anticipating fresh, rich experience. But he's not even there yet. He can only see Brunelleschi's great Duomo rising from the city, which crushes him with pleasure. As he rides into town his head starts to spin. Dante, Michelangelo, da Vinci all worked there; Lorenzo de' Medici established his powerful court there, which Stendhal believed to be the first since the reign of Augustus to make military prowess secondary to artistic achievement. European civilization was renewed here. His soul is helplessly revving up in predictable but worrying ways: "I found myself grown incapable of rational thought [and] surrendered to the sweet turbulence of fancy."

It's his first time in Florence, but Beyle has studied the street plan in advance and feels confident enough to leave behind his transport and all his belongings and explore the medieval catwalk streets. Making his way finally to the Church of Santa Croce—I once lived practically next door so I have some feeling for what he went through—he goes inside, sees Canova's effigy of Alfieri and the tombs of Michelangelo, Machiavelli, and Galileo. He's overwhelmed by the energy, by reimagined energy now laid to rest, and enjoys the exalted company: "What a fantastic gathering! The tide of emotion which overwhelmed me flowed so deep that it could scarce be distinguished from religious awe." It's testimony of physical unease as spiritual awakening. Religious awe induces visions and spirit-tremblings, it dissolves the ego and colonizes us.

A friar lets him into a chapel decorated with frescoes by the Baroque painter Baldassare Franceschini (or il Volterrano, after his birthplace Volterra), and when Beyle looks up to study the ceiling, he has an experience we recognize: "I underwent the profoundest experience of ecstasy I ever encountered through the painter's art. My soul was already in a state of trance. Absorbed in the contemplation of *sublime beauty*, I could perceive its very essence, feel the stuff of it under my fingertips. I had attained to that supreme degree of sensibility where *divine intimations* of art merge with the impassioned sensuality of emotion." When he leaves, his heart is racing, he's completely drained, feels faint, and has to sit on a bench to recover. He's knocked out by the Keatsian piercingness of all that beauty and by the ambition of it, which amount to the same thing. Every summer in Florence, tourists, Americans usually, suffer fits of what an Italian psychiatrist eventually identified as Stendhal syndrome. They get butterflies, feel dizzy or disoriented, succumb to anxiety attacks, and are generally overcome by the hard freight of beauty they're taking in. How many of us have had an authentic ecstatic religious experience or felt a sublime spiritual awe that makes us want to change our life? If we're suddenly broken down by beauty overloads that force us to submit to a palpable transcendence, we're bound to feel confused.

You don't have to go to Florence to have a Stendhal attack. Art writers spend a lot of time in museums, obviously, and develop high tolerances, but we can't stay fresh unless we stay in some way as softly vulnerable as any first-time tourist looking at the Manets in the Met or the Matisses at the Barnes Foundation. It can happen anywhere. I write about exhibitions in the Southland for the *San Diego Reader*, and sometimes I wander through the less than modest permanent collection at the San Diego Museum of Art just to be worked over by the goldenness of the golden cloak in El Greco's *St. Peter*, or by Ribera's weird double portrait of a child and crone—her leathery features look raked into the painting's surface, the babe's pasty face and head are grotesquely inflated. In a picture by some anonymous Netherlandish follower of Hieronymus Bosch, of Christ taken captive in the garden, the captor, whose ear a stubby, slope-nosed Peter has just cut off, is *biting* Peter's arm. The figures are all grotesques except Christ, as if the human condition he came to deliver them from is a derangement or disfigurement.

Art induces irrational states. That's one of its first pleasures. To describe the experience, we use the vocabulary of what's undifferentiated and devouring—we're *swamped* or *flooded* or *swarmed around* or *blown away*. Such a moment struck during one of my regular trips to New York. (I live in San Francisco and remind myself of something Clement Greenberg once said: "You gotta keep up!") I was beating the sidewalks, taking in big shows of Thomas Eakins, Gauguin, Joan Mitchell, and Greuze, and since I was uptown, though my energies were dropping fast and I was feeling overall bleary, I stopped by the Guggenheim to take in an anthology show of photographic, video, and digital imagery. It was there, after four days of taking in as much as I could stand, that I was struck down. The French installation artist Christian Boltanski had covered the walls of one gallery with hundreds of photographs—family snapshots, album images of families and Nazi soldiers, school class pictures, nudie magazine photos—illuminated by dim exposed light bulbs dangling so low from wires that they made a maze I had to navigate, a curtain to part and pass through. When banal snapshots from the Nazi era are set near blurry portraits of children—which we know from Boltanski's other work to be mostly faces of Jewish schoolchildren he pilfers from yearbooks—the sublime horrific-ness and hopeless bereavement are overwhelming. The more I looked, the shakier I became, until my head and stomach began to ache so much—I was already choked up enough to make a scene—that I had to get out and not go near a museum for the rest of my stay.

On my trip home I encountered a kind of cultural apoplexy that is our very own. Waiting in JFK for my flight to the Bay Area, I couldn't stop staring at a huge split screen that projected images of Africa over a vague strumming sound track, apparently the latest in environmental engineering to relax the weary traveler. No voice-over explained what I was watching: elephant herds stampeding or bathing, a leopard in a tree, clouds, unidentifiable tribal people making ceramics (to what purpose I had no clue). I looked away to scout the nearest bagel opportunity, and when I turned back, the pixilated African imagery had changed to indeterminable landscapes, sunsets, waterfalls, and there goes a *yacht* sailing merrily on a choppy gray-green sea. At

9 A.M. the lounge is crowded, but I'm the only malingerer ogling the screens. The turbo-fired surge of pictures, a derangement, was clearly designed as excitement to occupy but not engage the eye—it's imagery drained of meaning. I kept staring and started to get dizzy, my head ached, I had to sit down and concentrate on breathing. These weren't beauty loads inducing an irrational feeling of transport, they were a patterned connivance to take my mind—all our minds—*off* things. Things like check-in lines and bad coffee. As I walked to the Jetway, I had to look back at the video monitors, which like Eurydice's voice called with some mysterious otherworldly enticement: they had flopped from Africa and landscapes to a view of the New York skyline, then medieval castles, posh eighteenth-century French interiors, and bagpipers on parade. It filled the eye with specific images that weren't specific to any coherent reality. It trusted in our unthinking image-savviness and knew we have come to expect crafted images that have no meaning, which are so inauthentic that we never think to doubt their authenticity.

VINCENT

Artists express love in different ways. Delacroix in his journals can hardly contain himself—"How I love painting!"—and his shivering, explosive imagery gives that love its speed and textures. Ingres' work is an emblem of an unsplashy, inquisitive love for line and measure, gorgeously discreet. Van Gogh, who learned and took from both, made pictures, good and bad alike, that are devotional acts of love calling out to the things of the world. His form language, developed over relatively few years of extremely hard work, was the instrument of an aggressive piety before the world's disclosures. He educated himself in public. After drifting through jobs as an art dealer, schoolteacher, bookstore clerk, and missionary to miners, he committed himself to art when he was twenty-eight and went about making drawings and pictures as if art-making was a religious office recited under duress but joyfully. He wanted to turn his devotional mania into images with no residue of self-attentiveness. From early drawings to the vibrating paintings of his last years, his work had no hint of showiness or self-aware virtuosity. He was lucid most of the time and in control of his actions and choices, but he pitched himself into art with an almost deranged desire to give back to the world what the world had given him: impassioned existence. Many of his admirers take Van Gogh to be a magnificently pitiful beast of art who is somehow not entirely responsible for what he made. His several hundred letters offer the most excitable and aggrieved account we have of an artist's inner life. He says that in one self-portrait he looks like a dog. He's a dog to others, too. He imagines that his own parents, with whom he quarreled violently, see him as a "big rough dog . . . *And he barks so loud!*" The poet Rilke, who admired Van Gogh as a St. Francis of art, says of one self-portrait that "the painter looks shabby and tormented, almost desperate, but not devastated: the way a dog looks when it's had a rough time."

Van Gogh's famous simplicity—his sister-in-law refers to it repeatedly in her memoir—jumps from his letters with rude directness and ingenuousness. "The world only concerns me in so far as I feel a certain debt and duty toward it because I have walked that earth for thirty years, and, out of gratitude, want to leave some souvenir in the shape of drawings or pictures—not made to please a certain cult in art, but to express a sincere human feeling." The work wasn't a sectarian activity or profession; it was the fluid, harmonious exercise of an existence, and its subject was the fullness of existence. His art doesn't set itself at some invulnerable, ironic point apart from life. The landscapes, nocturnes, and flowers coil and oscillate toward some convergence, some impossible point of Oneness. But it's not a placid, "oriental" action. Cypress trees, compacted and wrapped in their protoplasmic energy, convulse and shear off toward the ether as if possessed of a will to bond with nature's other elements.

His painterly gestures were acts of driven reciprocity. We attribute our own secular disinterestedness to Van Gogh if we think of him as a modernist saint on a mission to investigate forms. His practice was mediated by predecessors large and small, but his impulses were as much religious and social as formal. He painted to offer his fellow earth residents some trace of redemption from the agonies of existence. We can feel desire in the arduous imaginative sympathy he showed his models: his intention wasn't to fashion a formal construct but to make an image of an actual existence. When his models didn't adequately respond to this pressure, he filled the insufficiency with his own suffering resources. We hear it in the unsettling mix of knowledge, righteousness, and ingenuousness in the letters. He writes his brother Theo that his work "lies in the heart of the people, that I must keep close to the ground, that I must grasp life at its deepest, and make progress through many cares and troubles."

When others speak of art as a *via crucis* they mean it in a secularized sense. Van Gogh's mission was more fanatical: he was artist of the Church Militant, the painter as pastoral warrior. Love's demands elemented his life and work. To Theo: "The clergymen call us sinners conceived and born in sin, bah! what dreadful nonsense that is. Is it a *sin* to love, to need love, not to be able to live without love? I think a life without love a sinful and immoral condition." (He was then enduring an unrequited love for a widow.) His righteous simplicity must have seemed a holy idiocy. The spastic riptide brushwork bears the rage of his love. Paint's mass, color, and texture were its substantiation. Again to Theo, in 1888 from Arles, after a bad episode: "I can very well do without God both in my life and in my painting, but I cannot, ill as I am, do without something which is greater than I, which is my life—my power to create."

And yet in his own wild way Van Gogh was canny enough to have a fair idea of how we would perceive him. "How can I be of use in the world?" he asks in a letter. "Can't I serve some purpose?" And we in turn utilize and exploit his passion. (Who would use Picasso this way?) We *expect* his work to serve us emotionally and morally. The artist we cozily call "Vincent," as he signed his pictures, scripted that response. He told Theo he wanted people to say that "he feels deeply, he feels tenderly, notwithstanding a so-called roughness, perhaps even because of it." He foresaw our proprietary and protective feelings toward him and the work, so in a sense it's he who owns us. We tend to read his career as an attempt to muscle down into forms, into raggedly sorrowing or pathologically ecstatic forms, the chaos incipient in pathos—pathos all over the place—for human nature and for nature's nature. His melancholy, the motor that ran hot and impelled the work, was an "active melancholy, which hopes and aspires and seeks, not a melancholy that despairs in stagnation and woe." He attacked the world and the canvas as one devotional gesture meant to evoke sacred presence as a fluid, jabbing, circulatory energy. In the stroke-by-stroke construction of the paintings we see the processual construction of selfhood, piece by piece, touch by touch, an "active melancholy" technique for crafting self-representation out of innumerable crude or confident recognitions of reality.

He tells Theo he's better off never really having learned to paint, because then nature could speak straight through him with minimal intervention. Being a porous medium let him create nervous pictorial meditations on eternity and on the natural order as a field of bristling circumstance. Like Millet, whom he revered, Van Gogh believed in "something on high." In the 1850s Millet wrote: "Nature yields herself to those who trouble to explore her, but she demands an exclusive love." That describes Van Gogh's devotionalism, though it wasn't only created nature he explored and loved in this way. The force of space and throbbing channels and fibers of objects are palpable even in his interiors. A floor, a bed, a table, a vase, a wall—even "denatured" stuff quivered with the divinity that lived in matter. He paints stars not as distant objects moving away from us, whose light always arrives so late, but as immanent presences, stirrings in consciousness. They are, like all material reality, fraught. He translates into pictorial feeling the ancient fact that the stars are divine beings. The stars, the firmament, covered the walls of his most impoverished rooms. His letters, like the pictures, swell with bold exquisite particulars. He saw the world as a viscous plenitude but also, sometimes in the same instant, as a scary vacancy. "Life itself is forever turning toward a man an infinitely vacant, discouraging, hopeless, blank side on which nothing is written, no more than on a blank canvas. But however vacant and vain and *dead* life may present itself, the man of faith, of energy, of warmth does not let himself be led astray by it."

In one of the letters Van Gogh talks about modeling not from clothes but from the soul, so that form-making takes the shape of temperament. ("One sees nature through one's own temperament.") In a small dog-faced self-portrait, he's wearing a creamy azure tie, felt hat, and badly fitting coat built up in narrow, heavy shingles of pigment. He's not really looking at us or himself, he's simply casting into strong forms a brutally intense temperament. The picture isn't saying "This is how I am," it's saying "Here is this thing." The 1888 *Self-Portrait as an Artist* shapes his figure out of the firmament's pulsing stuff. Rings and radiants of stabbing light swirl to create the head, so that the flesh looks as if it's expanding like space matter saddling back on itself. It's an image of an artist who can achieve explosive greatness but who may never mature.

Like Cézanne, Van Gogh made "saints" of his objects, but it's a fatigued sainthood. His vision of a pair of old shoes or clogs carves into them a history of wear and exhaustion—they seem intensely alive *because* they're empty, used up. His bedroom at Arles, a shrine decorated with the most austere and necessary tokens, isn't soulful local color, it's an unstable, trembling mass that bells outward toward the painter's testimonial eye like phantasmagoria, like a dream of things as essences. Combed coils of saturated light were Van Gogh's favorite forms for expressing recognitions of physical reality. In a picture of a wheat field, the grain is a sea of raked yellow crests scooping down one upon another. His nature is never a stilled scene, as it was for Corot. He makes the natural order as anxious and overriding a presence as his own presence in the self-portraits. The landscapes have a jumpy fervor. The nocturnes seethe. It's the language of someone who weeps for the world's sorrows but who has schooled himself to translate them into a brisk, excitable style. All is *vanitas* in his pictures of nature and the human figure, and all is love. Because he painted the natural world with such verve, it's curious that Van Gogh's animal pictures are so inert and illustrative. He made a painting of a crab on its back that is strangely affectless and mostly just self-instructive, and his *Flying Fox* is muddy and awkwardly drawn. This artist, who in portraits and landscapes could express with great accuracy his feeling for the way the transcendent throbs in the actual, became heavy-handed and crude when he tried to represent the animal world, probably because his desire for adequate likeness overwhelmed expressive ardor.

The process of educating himself, of pitching himself toward whatever possibilities beckoned, produced strange things like the grotesque *Skull of a Skeleton with Burning Cigarette* (campy noir book-cover art) and crowd-pleasing oddities like *The Courtesan,* a stiffly glamorous imitation of Japanese printmaking. One especially perverse picture is the *Pietà (after Delacroix)*. Delacroix, a dandified and not especially devout man, made biblical pictures that in their inventiveness and vigor are saturated with religious feeling. Van Gogh's picture is too plaintive in its pathos; the melodramatic modeling and glutinous color turn a feeling for sacred event into trivial hysteria. And it's instructive to see the effect on his growth by lesser painters like Anton Mauve and Jozef Israëls, whom he knew during his two years in The Hague and whose work he showered with encomia that most of us reserve for Rembrandt. His crawl space of a painting, *Potato Eaters,* with its shocking rendering of hunger as communal saintliness, was in part homage to a subject already treated by Israëls.

Van Gogh spent two years in the early 1880s in The Hague. He'd already been there in the early 1870s, working as a clerk-gofer—"Two years of black misery and hard work"—for an art dealer. He then went to work in the missionary field among miners in the Borinage in Belgium, where around 1878 he began drawing. After a short period in Brussels and a return home to Etten, where at Christmas in 1881 he quarreled so violently with his father that he had to leave, he returned to The Hague and thought of it as his second home. The Hague already had its own school. In the early 1870s painters like Anton Mauve, the senior eminence in Dutch painting and for a time Van Gogh's host and teacher, along with younger artists like Willem Maris and Jozef Israëls, were translating Barbizon plein-airism into a northern idiom. (To Theo: "A painting by Mauve, Maris, or Israëls expresses more, and more clearly, than nature itself.") By 1875 they were casually referred to as the Hague school, and it was this company of talents that the energetic, unformed, and no longer youthful Van Gogh entered. His first mission was to improve his drawing. He had small choice, since he couldn't afford oil paints and didn't like watercolor. Nature is already the deity to be worshipped.

Van Gogh brought to his new vocation the reformist ardor and spirit of social witness from his missionary years in the Borinage. Commissioned to produce a set of views of The Hague, then much in demand, he produced work so unmarketable that he got no further commissions: he was drawn to working-class neighborhoods, third-class waiting rooms, poorhouses, and other unofficial (and therefore unsavory) subjects. In an 1882 picture, a view of a ditch where women hang wash on a fence line, all we see of the prosperous Hague is the backs of houses in the distance. Van Gogh depicted working-class projects, thousands of which existed at the time (in one of them lived Sien Hoornik, the prostitute who became his partner), but which remained otherwise undocumented until they were photographed in the twentieth century. He toiled to make himself an artist and toil was one of his themes. Laundry women, peat haulers, potato grubbers, fisherfolk, sand diggers—these were the figures he drew during his Hague sojourn. The genre pictures of poor people the Hague school produced were mostly cozy and patronizing. Van Gogh had given up his social-religious activism but its energy fueled his training. He wasn't much interested in still life and, surprisingly, didn't fancy himself much of a landscape painter. The figure obsessed him. He sketched working people in large part because he couldn't afford sitters' fees. His 1882 drawing of Sien peeling potatoes is moving and unsentimental. Chinless, with large blocky hands, the homely Sien's attractiveness is rendered in the concentrated devotion to her small task. She and her labor aren't patronized by style. Van Gogh's earnest, rough-and-ready draftsmanship frees his subject into unexpected feeling tones. While he learned the analytical dynamics of drawing from studying the work of his contemporaries—from Mauve he learned pictorial construction and painterly technique—he didn't borrow their preoccupation with calculated, academic effects.

The 1885 *Potato Eaters* was modeled on Israëls's genre scenes of families gathered around a frugal meal. Israëls's pictures are muted, almost buttery, and diffidently atmospheric. In 1902, when Van Gogh's reputation was growing, Israëls titled one of his genre scenes *Potato Eaters*. The faces and rough homespun of Israëls's peasants gathered around their common bowl are rendered in long-streaked, purplish flesh tones. The picture is well-built and purposeful but has none of the frontal immediacy and rude intrusiveness of view—an ungenteel familiarity—that gives Van Gogh's treatment its grotesque candor and makes it an expression of communal appetite and want. In his eager, febrile way, Van Gogh took whatever he needed from whatever source. The knobby melodramatic modeling of the face of the woman pouring coffee in *Potato Eaters* came from an engraving by M. W. Ridley called *The Miner*, which Van Gogh found in one of the back issues of the English periodical *The Graphic*—he admired its illustrations for their stark crystalline draftsmanship, their panicked high relief, the alert sympathetic witness to suffering and circumstance that he wanted to achieve in his own work. Most good artists are essentially contrary, or off in some way. Van Gogh set out to make himself into a rather conventional artist of social conscience and was intent on mastering techniques which, as exercised by the Hague school at least, had no propulsive effect in the history of modern art. His genius was of a kind that put conventional technique and customary preoccupations to the task of overmastering themselves and being deranged by visionary desire.

POCKETBOOK AND SAUERKRAUT

I

I didn't know I was a member of the working class until I no longer was. In the dense South Philadelphia Italian neighborhood where I grew up, there were no class distinctions because we were all one socioeconomic group. The few men with skilled trades made out a little better than those like my father whose lack of training qualified them at best for low-level general maintenance jobs. The skilled workers might own a bigger TV set or have a taller fir tree in their parlors at Christmas, and the only boy who owned a football was the son of a workingman employed in the mysterious and relatively new field called electronics, clean work, the only kind of work we saw advertised on TV in General Electric commercials. Progress is our most important product, it said. The sense of that slogan meant nothing to me as a child, but the tune the words made, the canter of that cadence, held in my mind as a beautiful pattern.

One street down, across Twenty-first Street, on the next block of Watkins, lived the only people spoken of as a different, inferior class. The black working people and their children rarely crossed over into our neighborhood. Though physically closer to us than any other group, in language they were demonized and made the most remote and adversarial; ethnic and racial tags made up our richest vocabulary. As tribes have many names for the most critical presence in their communal life—twenty words for snow or river or salmon—we all had words to fix and set apart the others. The black boys who sometimes crossed over in gangs and jumped us would chant the names: Guinea, Boon, Greaser, Whitey, Wop. And we had names for them: Spook, Rubberhead, Jigaboo, Spade, *Mul'*. Where did "Boon" come from? What southern dialect turned *melanzana*, "eggplant," into *mulagnam'*, shortened to *mul'* and pronounced "mool"? I loved the loose, slippery textures of those words as much as I clenched inside to hear them used. But I also sensed that to reject the language of the tribe was to risk rejecting its identity and reality in the world. Reject the words and you were in some way killing off your own people, casting yourself into an exile of prideful superiority. There grew in me a child's conviction that language was a locked box in which were stored the most irrational, alienating, and violent voices. The most puzzling thing of all was the discrepancy between the censoring otherness that words attached to our working-class black neighbors and the reality my eye took in. Our block was clean but colorless and drab, without ornament: redbrick row houses, granite front steps, and a single large sycamore. One block down, however, they had planters in front of their houses, more trees, too, and window boxes that splashed the distant air with wonderful colors. On our block, I hardly ever saw fresh flowers indoors or out. For signs of joy, for Nature, I looked across the Twenty-first Street divide to that *other* place.

Among my people an awareness of ethnic separateness was more important than socioeconomic or political identity. Non-Italians were *americani*, except blacks and Jews. They weren't Americans, either. From the man who worked at G.E. we would hear about black coworkers, whom he spoke of with respect and goodwill; he was also the only man in the neighborhood to go out on strike. Most of the others feared a strike because they had too much at risk and tended to be suspicious anyway of anyone outside the family-neighborhood orbit. The G.E. father, however, drew mysterious power from the group, from the mass of workers acting as one entity, one will. The refusal to work, walking off the job, was so out of keeping with the mentality of my neighborhood that to my young mind it seemed at once heroic and insane.

We know ourselves in part by the misrepresentations others make of us. Years after I'd left Philadelphia, someone I knew pretty well but to whom I'd said little about my early years assumed I grew up in an Italian culture rich with peasant traditions, Verdi on the phonograph, flowers everywhere, Old Master reproductions on the wall, tomatoes ripening in the backyard.

In my house there were no flowers, no music other than top ten pop, and no images except for devotional tchotchkes and boiled black-and-white images on TV. There's no peasantry in my background, only village laborers and tradesmen (and, a few generations back, a priest who left his property holdings to the prostitute who bore his child; a professional gambler; a racketeer; and a bigamist who became a boom-to-bust coffee plantation tycoon somewhere in South America). Another friend assumed I came from an anarcho-syndicalist background, as if all immigrant laborers were political kin to Sacco and Vanzetti. There was, in fact, never a mention of working classes. People talked mostly about us Italians and all the *americani*. Until I went to college, where I was taught that there has been no determinant class system in America comparable to those in European nations like Italy, with historical distinctions between peasant and landowner, subproletariat and proletariat, petit bourgeois and aristocrat, I'd hardly met anyone who spoke differently from me, and though I didn't know it then, I understood in time that one purpose of American education was to detach me, or enable me to detach myself, from what I was finally learning to call "the working class" into which I was born.

My class awareness, such as it was, came packed in words and speech. I still repeat to myself the rhyme we learned as kids:

> I made you look, you dirty crook,
> I stole your mother's pocketbook.
> I turned it in, I turned it out,
> I turned it into sauerkraut.

The lines live in the same zone and continuity of my consciousness as certain passages in poems and movies. Their words compose a *mysterium sanctum* where meaning lies in wait for initiates, and where language bleeds together conversation, doggerel, and formal elegance into one way of speech. But you can study, make sacrifice, burn incense, and still not be enlightened, for meaning is also sometimes a surprising gift, a sentence whose rhythms spring like a trap and catch you. At that sanctuary Nimrod, Babel's architect, is the spectral custodian, always there to break sense into incoherence. But it was, is, my true place. Outside, vendors sold hoagies and pizza steaks and lemonade. L-e-m-o-n-a-d-e had all the sweetness of sound I expected of the thing. Except that it wasn't really lemonade. Only in my teens did I learn that what we called lemonade was really lemon water ice. Lemonade was, for Americans, a *drink*! I was set straight by a high school pal, a lawyer's son. I made you look, you dirty crook. My real learning was about the executive power of language to reveal, enchant, disguise, and transgress. Who knows what "education" was being buzzed around my head by the sisters in grade school and the priests in high school? Turning someone's mother's pocketbook into sauerkraut was a power as outlandish and severe in its illusion as Harpo's power at the stringboard. Fantastical and sleight of hand, words in patterns had a lightness and buoyant canniness that my culture of labor either had no time for or disdained outright. What my culture did give me was a sense—a tactile, mineral sense—of language as the embodiment of contingency. And I think I also absorbed other qualities that have served me as a poet, a tenacity and a stupefied willfulness to make words answerable to the densities of consciousness.

But language, of course, wasn't so nicely patterned or cut to satisfying forms. That's not how I experienced it. It was swampy, crazily shadowed, and veined with unintelligible matter. Its flashes and zigzags and curls pulled me in. Wordplay baffled me. When I was a kid, one of my uncles, answering the door when I knocked, said: "So what can I sue you for?" Why would he want to sue me? What had I done? Was he joking? Why joke about taking away everything I owned? My own uncle! *Sue you for*—force you, sure— use your four—O Sue, for you! I still suffer anxiety about the incipient babble in sentences. It has made me an unstable and easily confused reader of poetry, and a writer of poems whose lines feel as if they're breaking down as soon as they come into a pattern of sense. The anxiety leaked very naturally into my speech as well, so that even now if I'm not attentive it will turn into a slur or mumble, and I'm terrified to speak *ex tempore*. The boys in my high school came from different neighborhoods, from Two Street, Grays Ferry, and Ninth and Carpenter, but nearly all came from backgrounds like my own. In college—St. Joseph's, a Jesuit school—I met boys from other backgrounds and places. Some had accents, from the South or Massachusetts or New York, but their speech didn't have the snarly, abrasive candor that sounded so clearly in the tones of Philadelphia working-class boys like myself. I was at ease, and could play the fiction of not speaking with an accent, only when I acted in plays. Otherwise, my bad nerves, uncertainty, and Nimrod anxiety made me too intense. I read with gusto Yeats's remarks in his *Autobiographies* about mastering the rhetorical arts and overcoming shyness. But my culture was massively different from his, and I certainly had no ambitions as a public person; I only wanted to break words and my own speech clear of their roughly shaped origins in my culture.

It did no good anyway. I was reading my Yeats while working long summer hours loading shipping crates with car doors, windshields, and wheels at a Ford Motor Company depot, or else working swing shift at the circuit-breaker factory where by day my mother (widowed several years before) worked on an assembly line. I read Yeats's approval of a remark in Villiers de l'Isle-Adam's *Axel's Castle:* "Live? Our servants will do that for us." A society or class that uses servants was, to my nineteen-year-old mind, candyland. To be at ease to do "the real work" of reading and writing! It was foolishness, but I've never quite given up that illusion, though I haven't given in to it, either. Sauerkraut and lemonade. Sour lemons aid the Krauts. For you, Sue, I sure can do. Then one night I met a Yeatsian lady, a Main Line sort of Yeatsian lady. For a few years after college I worked a succession of menial jobs. One summer I parked cars at a band shell in Fairmount Park. One evening, a middle-aged couple in a luxury car ignored my directions and parked in what I soon learned was their favorite (and therefore privileged) spot under a tree. "You remember where we like to park," he said, "and we'll remember you." Confused because tips and unearned privileges had never figured in my previous work experience, I tried to cover my nerves with what I thought were amiable remarks about that evening's Debussy program. The lady, elegantly silent till then, turned to her husband: "What is this person saying? Can *you* understand him?" I quit the job that night. I was twenty-two and about to leave Philadelphia for good. I knew that Yeats was thinking metaphorically, as was Villiers, but only in part. With their aristocratic ambitions, their cult of symbolist disembodiment, and their enthrallment to residual forms of nobility wherever they might be found, both poets were writing fact. I couldn't shake off so suddenly what I was reading and absorbing with such hunger—Yeats seemed a poet who could conquer any tone, speak intensely and formally as one person to another, bring over philosophy into the feeling life of poetry, and his Irishness made him seem archaically foreign—but I also knew that I didn't want servants doing my living for me, in metaphor or in fact, and that I didn't want servants of any kind.

In the early 1970s, a few years after my encounter with the Yeatsian concert-goer, I went to live in Italy, where my education in class distinctions continued. It was a tense time. The protests of 1968 and the years following seemed to have politicized nearly every relation in society, from office to schoolroom to kitchen. The Christian Democrats remained the majority party in the coalition government, but for some years the Communist Party under Enrico Berlinguer's leadership had been pursuing its *compromesso storico*, the historic compromise that would lead to the Communist Party's sharing in the coalition. Berlinguer's "communism with a human face" was building its power base not only among the working class but also among the managerial and professional classes. Bologna, where I lived for two years, was a specimen in the experiment. The scene of student and political violence in the 1960s, it was under Communist leadership in the 1970s and becoming the best administered, most congenial and stable local government in the country.

Several of my friends and clients (I survived mainly on private lessons and commercial translation work) were businessmen, professors, and doctors, who voted Communist or Socialist. I lived in a crumbling sixteenth-century tenement that housed working-class families and tradespeople. The aged lady who lived on the top floor shared a minuscule apartment—there was no central heating in our building—with her nephew; together they operated a produce stand at the local outdoor market. My middle-class friends discussed politics with great seriousness. They fervently supported the struggle of the working class; they also had servants to clean their houses, prepare their meals, and nanny their children. When I said that it seemed a contradiction for Socialists and Communists to keep servants, my friends agreed, for they suffered the contradiction of class privilege versus class affiliation. It confused me to realize that they exercised political passion out of ideological conviction and sympathy, not out of material necessity or inherited grievance. (During my years in Bologna, a few of my friends realized they couldn't live the contradiction and so released their servants.) They had grown up petit bourgeois. In the evening, I would come home from political conversations in spacious, well-furnished apartments and have to help the vegetable monger carry bags up four flights of stairs to her two-room garret.

I was a sort of specimen, a true child of the working class (glazed with an American ingenuousness that Italians spotted at once), but I was trying to make my way as a poet, translator, and critic, which placed me closer to the professional and culture-elite classes than to the working class. I didn't fit the picture Italians had of the American social system, where class lines were so liquid and so frequently dissolved under the pressure of "opportunity" that the children of cement-finishers and pipe fitters could become lawyers, surgeons, even accountants. (My college's strongest program was Food Marketing.) My literary ambitions brought respect from my successful friends and from my upstairs neighbor. I had read Pound's remark that in Europe no shame adhered to a writer who was poor. My situation caused me both to see and in a small way experience the contradictions and guilt that existed within and among the social classes in Italy. My own youthful experience seemed blessedly simple by contrast.

One night a few of us went to the premiere of Pasolini's film *The Canterbury Tales*. "We have to see it right away," they said. "It'll be confiscated as soon as it opens." When we left the theater, *carabinieri* were waiting in their cars and closed the movie that night. Pasolini had a certain claim on Bologna; he'd gone to high school and university there, though he hailed from the Friuli region and lived most of his adult life in Rome. In the early 1970s he was at the peak of his international fame as a filmmaker and had been for years a provocative figure in Italian culture and politics. Pasolini came to fame as a poet in the late 1950s with *The Ashes of Gramsci*. Antonio Gramsci, cofounder of the Italian Communist Party, was tried and imprisoned for many years under the Fascist regime. During his imprisonment he kept voluminous notebooks that contained seminal ideas about crafting a peculiarly Italian communism rooted in local needs and a locally evolved economy. During his imprisonment he instructed fellow prisoners (some of them hard-core criminals) in literature and history. Though a child of the petit bourgeoisie—his father was a civil administrator of some kind in Sardinia—Gramsci was preoccupied with the struggles of the new industrial working classes and their place in an emergent communist society.

In the poem, Pasolini visits Gramsci's grave in Rome's Protestant Cemetery, where Shelley and other foreigners, mostly English, are buried. The carefully tended grounds and gardens are to Pasolini an image of patrician privilege. Beyond the cemetery lies the rough working-class slum of Testaccio. Pasolini, child of a career military man and a schoolteacher, positions himself between the cemetery's refined appointments and Testaccio's messy workshops, between the historical imagination of Gramsci (Italian hero buried among foreigners, man of prose, strategist for the reorganization of industrial society) and the speculative imagination of Shelley (English patrician in self-imposed exile, man of poetry, visionary of revolutionized consciousness). Pasolini positions himself in the middle, isolated by his own uncertainty, "Between hope / and my old distrust," between the hope for freedom of appetite he hears in the din of Testaccio and his old distrust of his petit bourgeois origins. Gramsci is a model of rigor in rejecting the allure of materialist culture and the exploitive relation to working-class people that capitalist culture is built on. But Pasolini, attracted sexually and ideologically to Testaccio, also values material comforts, the remnants of the "bourgeois evils / [that] wounded my bourgeois self." (In later years, young men recognized the cruising Pasolini by the luxury cars he drove.) He knows that Gramsci, like many of the foreigners buried around him, succeeded by force of will, self-discipline, and intensity of purpose, and that the workers of Testaccio survive by smarts and sweat, always a step away from chaos, tossed by momentary passions. But as a poet and intellectual Pasolini occupies his own disconsolate, ineffectual dead zone.

To write poetry is to transform passion into a symbol world, bringing over the quick of the senses into annals of lore and image-hoarding. The intellectuality of poetry doesn't return a poet to the source, to Testaccio's fevers. We take ourselves out of life to speak more passionately of life. Pasolini knows that his clothes, though threadbare from use, are the kind working-class people covet. He loves their vulgar taste for glamorous shop windows with their "crude splendors" even while his own tastes force him into an ironic regard. (When he cruised working-class neighborhoods he often changed down from his normal workaday attire to tight polyester blouses and ankle boots.) He loves the workers' hunger for life's passions in part because he has had to school himself in the reflective delay crucial to poetry. His poem is a cry at his own helplessness in the middle, that despised place, between Testaccio and the lovely gardens of death.

Pasolini never really left that middle zone, the place of contradiction. Soon after the major critical successes of *The Ashes of Gramsci* and his two novels, *A Violent Life* and *The Ragazzi*, he became an increasingly controversial filmmaker and cultural critic for major newspapers. With success came material rewards. I recognize him as the sort of artist whose political consciousness was stoked by his desire to migrate to a class to which he would never choose to belong. If born into the working class, he would have howled to set himself free of its censures and maledictions. He was fervently loyal to it because he was free to visit that life, not obligated to live it. His sexual privilege was his freedom to pick up and enjoy boys among whom he was not destined to live. But he was also an artist unafraid to live out his contradictions in public. During the violent demonstrations of 1968, Pasolini published a poem in which he sided with the policemen fighting students, because the police were children of the working class, with limited opportunities in life. The students were, like himself, children of the middle class and spoiled by the entitlements a hierarchical society seeks to preserve and protect. The truly revolutionary gesture, the authentic Gramscian gesture, was to support the police in their conflict against the preservers of class privilege. Pasolini in effect claimed his own Marxist pedigree as justification for supporting traditional law enforcement.

The unmentioned presence in *The Ashes of Gramsci* is Keats, also buried in the Protestant Cemetery. Yeats described him correctly as a stable keeper's son too much enchanted by sensuous delight. But Keats was also, most of all, the poet of the senses' disclosures. Poetry for him was pure possibility, a medium for sensuous anticipation and surprise. He certainly showed his hungers—Yeats described him as a boy with his nose pressed to a sweet-shop window—and didn't agonize over his class origins as did Pasolini, Shelley, and Yeats, for whom the passionate life was to be found elsewhere, in Testaccio, in a classless society, in the rooms of great houses. Middle-class contradictions are no anxiety for an artist born into the working classes. The great anxiety is to separate oneself from those origins, escaping their violent censures and intolerance for the life of the imagination. Keats's career was a pursuit of the sensuous immediacy and hauntedness of the flesh that Pasolini anguishes over in *The Ashes of Gramsci*. For Pasolini, as for so many artists of the middle class, passion becomes "problematical." (For some it becomes a high-toned dilemma: one sees ludicrous poems today with ludicrous titles like "The Mind-Body Problem," "The Problem with My Heart," and "The Problem of Passion.") Artists born to the working class face their own temptations, one of which is to reduce memory and experience to local color or cult object. There will always be a sentimental market for blue-collar verities, alley cat wisdom, and tenement transcendentalism. Just as there are markets for exotic otherness, ethnic enchantments, and "subculture" opportunisms. I try not to let my work be dyed too richly or flamboyantly with Mercutio's red impetuosity. Contrariness may be the most enduring habit passed on by my working-class culture; its formal consequence is a barely sustained coherence of passion and idea.

3

In the prose stylists I was reading in my twenties—Edward Dahlberg, Camus, Nietzsche, John Jay Chapman—I found a value, expressed mostly in political or moral terms, that I was pursuing in poetry: the sensuous shapeliness of form governing and measuring ungovernable passion. I felt words to be in a constant semisolid state, however fixed their etymologies. They weren't vehicles for stating passion, they were themselves the rapid uneven pulse and texture of passion. But somewhere along the way I also became persuaded, I don't know how, that the objects of the world cannot be owned by figures of consciousness. It's probably my deepest political conviction that there is in the things of the world an essential stilled singularity that cannot be expropriated even by the mastering forms of the imagination. The enchantments of representation are not true magic. Poetry doesn't transform the world, it embodies the particular acts and feelings of being in the world. The things of the world resist words and wordiness.

I must have experienced poetry from the beginning as an attempt to fuse and discriminate at the same time, in one sentence, to blend into words the unsorted particulars of experience, and to make words not report the conflict but enact it. The figures of consciousness played out in a poem weren't decorative or idly pleasurable but rhetorical, litigious, Mercutial, sometimes disablingly or obscurely so. (I sometimes think that working-class Roman Catholics feel the nerves of Puritanism more immediately and practically than any Protestant New Englander.) That impatience has carried over into my critical judgments. I don't like poetry with slyly built-in mechanisms of self-justification (Frost is our American master of this: equivocal wisdom born of equivocal humility), and I dislike the sentimentality of all-purpose sorrowing. I'm impatient with anyone who would define me or my work in terms of my origins. Intellectual discourse has been full of talk about hegemonic structures or principles, and one of these is class. Begin with the determinant factor of class, the argument runs, and all other qualities will follow from that. No poet can afford to think that way because it's the technique of a mind that fears the messy particulars of embodiment and believes temperament to be an accident of language rather than a part of its genetic structure.

Class isn't determinant, but it is formative. When I ran my pocketbook-sauerkraut rhyme through my head or hummed "Better Buy Birds Eye" until its sense melted into the rhapsodic swells Poe believed to be poetry's purest music, when I studied the tiny reproductions of paintings in grade school Picture Study books or read through encyclopedia articles and poems by Poe and Edna St. Vincent Millay and Vachel Lindsay at the free library, they weren't a richness beyond my poverty (we weren't poor, we just had no money, and there were few books around) or a promise of transport beyond my means. They were enchanting forms, mysterious shapes that had a density of ordered feeling of which life itself seemed a rough sketch or study. My own day-to-day life felt like constant bad weather inside my head, of anger and sullenness, hilarity and melancholy, with no placid middle zones, just as there seemed to be no middle temperaments among the boys I played with, who were either predatory, coarse, manipulative, and crazy or quiet, nervous, anxious to please, and in jeopardy. In time, the poetry I wanted to write would be one without middle zones, without a sustained discursive middle range or plain presentational balance. I didn't want to sound like Tennyson, sonorous, dignified, and responsible. Browning was closer: capable of the most exquisite lyric effects but also twitchy and volatile and impatient. I'm touched by Henry James's description of him reading his poems aloud in a way that suggested he hated them, biting and twisting the words, anxious, unsatisfied, inflamed by their very existence.

People in my neighborhood were scrupulously honest with one another, but the men felt no guilt pinching things from their workplace. My first writing materials—it's laughably grandiose to call them that—were hot goods. Like many children, I scribbled away at stories and plays. The miserable wage my father earned at Temple University Hospital—he'd gone straight to work after grade school, then gotten drafted—was offset by small items cadged by a friend of his in "Supplies." Bolts of colored twine, paper clips, staples, gleaming Ticonderoga pencils, index cards, scratch pads and legal pads and letter files—portable things easily smuggled home but, in a household like ours, almost completely useless. Paper clips to attach what to what? We had no "documents," kept no records, wrote and received no letters, never made shopping lists. The stationery was a weird bonus, a little windfall that brought no real benefit because it answered no real need. Except mine, which was secret. I now had materials. Several years ago, long after my father's death, on a visit home I rooted through some boxes in the cellar and found remnants of my childhood stash, and I've put them to use—lacquered yellow pencils asleep in their slip boxes, legal pads warped and browned at the edges, grease pencils with their slick pull-string coils. A fair amount of what I've written has been done on hot stuff, stolen materials that were, in the conscience of my people, worker's compensation.

2

WORK

One of the stranger memories of my childhood is the textured space that seemed to surround men on my block as they went back and forth to work. To us children, "at work" meant a place, not just an activity, a temporary habitat outside the neighborhood. Work was the surround that absorbed them every morning and restored them to us at day's end, a little transfigured by dust or grease, hands smelling of borax, breath beery or whiskied. And they carried that aura. In the mornings it should have been crisp, but something careworn and irredeemable wrapped itself about them. None ever seemed happy or expectant, as if work, the need and the duty of it, was a mineral substance they wore like a coat. It told me that work was never a lightness and gaiety, but something gravid, earthborn and earthbound. The departures were built on ritual morning preparations: the clatter of cups on saucers, the gurgle of coffee perking, the familiar cadence of feet down the stairs, the gulps and sluicing of water through old plumbing. If life's ordinary rhythms were repeated faithfully, they were charms that helped sustain a household. Observe the ritual and you were safe against most disruptions caused by your own laziness and stupidity. If bad fortune wanted you, it would have to come get you. But break the ritual, fail in some regular observance out of weariness or distraction, and a job would be jeopardized, and therefore a household, extending to grandparents and possibly a bachelor aunt or uncle. Fool with the rigors of habit and you became your own bad luck.

I had no sense of the daily humiliations many of them suffered in their jobs. Some had the hot, sharp intelligence that intellectuals envy, but advanced education, even high school, wasn't available to them, so many made their way as unskilled laborers. They seemed not so much beaten or embarrassed by their work as numbed to a silence their children could hardly pierce. They weren't heroic, either, though it's the tendency of those who learn about the struggle of material existence from books to either ennoble workers or "demythologize" them. Hannah Arendt says that since the nineteenth century we've glorified labor as the source of all values. For us children, the great thing was that our fathers worked with their hands, built big things with big tools, drove loud trucks, put things together on assembly lines, or mixed explosive chemicals in oceanic proportions. They mended ship fittings in the Navy Yard, tarred high roofs, laid brick for doctors' offices, mounted pistons on locomotives, poured concrete for skyscrapers and walked out to the edge of girders forty stories up, right there at the edge of nothing at all.

My memory is colored by what I now know them to have done. The chemicals man, in my mind's eye, always looks unnaturally scrubbed, his face blanched or parched, and all around his stiff posture—stiffened in expectation of some explosion or concussion—the air is tinted sulfurous yellow. And the man whose job was to young boys the most exciting, who broke pavement with a jackhammer, bore a chalky cowl around his head, as if the job had cast a permanent proprietary veil. He had a sailor's rolling gait, checking his balance after a jittery day. Only one had no aura, who was only what he was. Already remote for living at the far end of the block, he walked the entire length of the street morning and evening; the promenade past our houses seemed part of his job. His distinction—and it may be this that rubbed out the aura—was the shirt he wore. A bright white shirt seen in fever, in daylight, will make your head swim. His, day after day, had that hallucinated candor. The shirt had no creases (I remember best spring and summer days, when everyone was in shirtsleeves), which meant he couldn't afford to send it to the laundry or chose not to. His collar was always open and starched. I never knew for sure what he did. Though he lived on our street, his son never played in our games. The women sometimes spoke in quickened breaths about "City Work," meaning government. He was probably a civil servant who could get by without a necktie but was expected to wear that white vestment. In a neighborhood filled with handsome southern Italians, he had a movie star's baked good looks and was trimmer than the others, not quite as square and planted. He was also the only adult ever to strike in anger a child not his own, an event that nearly caused a riot and became legend for years. The legend's heraldic sign was the shirt.

As children organize the mixed facts the world blasts at them into classes of related things, into metaphoric families, I constructed a class called "Working Men." My neighbor in the famous shirt didn't belong. He was slotted into a mongrel sort occupied by two other men. (It was always and only men, in that sort of neighborhood in the 1950s; the only woman to hold a job also divorced her husband and "broke the block" by selling her house, next door to ours, to a black family.) One was the angel idiot, a stricken holy creature in his late twenties, whose hungry beauty seemed traced by a Filippino Lippi. Because he was epileptic, he didn't work and wasn't expected to. He became the kind of friend and protector to neighborhood children that their fathers, away from the house all day and many in the corner taproom till late evening, could never be. His demon, the sudden scrambling of the body's electricity that turned him into an inexplicably self-punishing creature, pardoned him from the world of work. But that torment was also his ethereal element, the Ariel in him: when he lay convulsed on the ground, he seemed least earthbound. His disease freed him. That seemed to me a horrible yet desirable privilege.

The other exception to my class of workers was a smiling, snappily dressed young man from a large family, the only one of several sons who didn't work. Much later, his image became confused in my mental gallery with the "fallen brother" in Visconti's *Rocco and His Brothers*, Simone, my grandfather's name (and mine), but by that time I'd also found a sharper clarification of work and workers in Paul Nizan's writing and Lewis Hine's photographs. My neighbor, at any rate, did no work because he was a gangster. All the adults knew this and were shamed by it, though I think the shame was mixed with envious anger. The gangster genius had all the fruits of work and luck—beautiful suits, good shoes, his own auto, friends who dressed as well as he—without working. Like my tormented Ariel and the foreigner in the white shirt, the gangster exempt from work was unnatural, a gorgeous freak. Each in his own way was a monster whose aberration accentuated the norms of habit that ruled our own lives.

Paul Nizan was a son of the railroad. His father rose through the ranks during the great expansion of the French railway system at the end of the nineteenth century, advancing from the "low" position of engineer to the more prestigious levels of lower management. Nizan came of age between the big wars and, like his friends Sartre and Camus, became a political writer of all trades—novelist, essayist, polemicist. *Antoine Bloyé*, published in 1933, is the novel that established his small but controversial reputation. It expresses with angry clarity the structures of habit and how one destiny is determined, and ill fortuned, by the conjunction of habit and a certain kind of economy. The structures of habit are really overlayerings of desire, palimpsest chronicles of the unhappiness which in turn replenishes habit and gives it even stricter control over life. Habit, while it seems to represent convenience and necessity, hides and seals away from us the anarchy of desire; it wrestles anarchy into daily repetitions.

Nizan introduces the story of Antoine Bloyé, another son of the railroad, with an epigraph from Marx's *The German Ideology:* "If communism is to put an end both to the 'cares' of the bourgeois and the needs of the proletarian, it is self-evident that it cannot do this without putting an end to the cause of both, 'labor.'" This contradicts a remark he's made a few pages earlier: "Men begin to distinguish themselves from animals when they begin to produce their means of subsistence." Hannah Arendt, in *The Human Condition*, describes the equivocation: "The fact remains that in all stages of his work [Marx] defines man as an *animal laborans* and then leads him into a society in which this greatest and most human power is no longer necessary." (Arendt's critique reflects her belief in labor as a celebrative participation in nature's processes and repetitions.) Marx evidently intended the emancipation from labor to be the emancipation from necessity. In the early *Economic and Philosophic Manuscripts*, he emphasized that labor is the expression of a human being's "sensuous nature." In the course of his life, Antoine Bloyé rises from laborer to manager, and in the process surrenders the opportunity to engage his sensuous nature in work.

Nizan's description of Antoine's daily office routine catches the ambiguity of habit—it sustains and reduces us, so do we celebrate or condemn it?

> Each morning he went to his office; he hung up his umbrella or his
> overcoat. Winter came and then summer; first the season of derby hats,
> then the season of straw hats, of panamas. He sat down, lit a cigarette,
> and went and opened the door of the neighboring office as soon as

he heard the sounds of a man, coughing, footsteps, a slight whistle, snatches of humming, the heavy sound of a body depositing its weight in an armchair. This meant the engineer had arrived.

That dull march of parallel phrases enacts what Nizan calls the "cotton wool" of habit. It protects, it softens the shock of the world, but it also packs us into a self-justifying indifference toward all that looms outside the laminations of habit. It's the most available vaccine against the contagion of political activism. Habit domesticates necessity so that we don't feel helpless to its demands. In Marx's ideal society, if the need to labor is dissolved, so are its fixed regularities. In a new society people will be able to "do this today and that tomorrow, who hunt in the morning, go fishing in the afternoon, raise cattle in the evening, are critics after dinner, as they see fit, without ever becoming hunters, fishermen, shepherds or critics." But if we give up habit, we give up the illusion of controlling circumstance. This sounds a little quaint in a post-Communism global economy, but the personal relevance of the freedom *to* work being freedom *from* work is still a bitterly alive question.

But Nizan's sympathies are stretched thin. He wants a Marxist formulation of class problems, but he shows an artist's loyalty to a suffering individual who isn't so much a casualty of capitalism as he is a powerful sensuous nature incapable of articulating his desires. Although Antoine doesn't know what happiness is, he knows he wants it. As a young man he hates the poverty he sees around him, but he doesn't think to change or understand it, he just wants to escape it. He sees from his father's work as a porter that a capitalist economy traps you in a job of everlasting repetitions. The sour irony is that in order to escape that submissiveness, Antoine enters the middle class, where he's even more trapped than his father because more implicated in an economic structure whose power he cannot share.

Digging and hacking the earth is a child's most powerful form of play. Even though my neighborhood was covered over with concrete and asphalt, we used to dig with sticks or knives in puny sidewalk cracks, methodically refilling our ditch-work. Children may be charmed by stories of idle fairies performing good deeds, but they are compelled and deeply swayed by tales of dwarfs who go off each day to pick and hammer mines. The only man whose job we children envied, and which we mimicked in our play, was the jackhammer man. I've seen my daughter and her friends break bricks with a hammer, crush the shattered bits into powder, bag it as if it were a precious mineral, then stir it into water. With the brick-dust impasto they drew pictures of houses. While breaking bricks—they were soon into mass production—they sang "I've Been Working on the Railroad." As if the rhythms of bodies at work, the claiming and use of earth's stuff, breaking down its forms so that it might be transformed, were all carried out in obedience to some primordial metabolic cadence.

But that's play. Concentrated, passionate, repetitive, *and* buoyant, unobliged, with no material relation to any society larger than that of children at play. Children working in real mines left no trace, but they had their chronicler in Lewis Hine, who recorded the contradictions of their work. In 1908 Hine quit high school and went to work as a photographer for the National Child Labor Committee to document the hideous working conditions in West Virginia's coalfields. Breaker boys, kids who sat fourteen hours a day six days a week bent over chutes separating slag from coal, were paid seventy-five cents a day. The shabbily dressed children in Hine's picture "Breaker Boys in Coal Chute" stare boldly at the camera. The few bits of exposed flesh, especially the gleaming knuckles and pale discs around the eyes, are impoverished instances of light in the gloom. That light is provoked by Hine's interrogating flash—the sole electrical fixture is dead. The only natural light is a brief exhalation of sunshine stoppered in the shed's window. In that strangely composed moment when the boys turn from their job, they look mineralized, half-transformed into the material of their labor. The eyes that look so candidly at us seem as yet untouched, the remaining untransformed part, as if the illumination of mind shining there was the only energy preserving them from being darkened by work's gravity.

Twenty-five years later, Hine has gone from the underground to the heavens and is photographing high-steel workers raising the Empire State Building. He saw in them—his "Skyboys"—the soul of early youth at a different stage of industrial civilization. Earth's mined products are now made over into towering architectonic forms; their use has been taken up and transformed by the imagination. The darkling breaker boys have grown and gone out, *up*, into the air. The most compelling image in the Skyboy series is the one most catalogs call "Icarus." A worker is bracing a cable with his extended right arm while his left clenches the cable for support.

His articulated forearm muscles imitate the cable's ropiness. At his feet is a huge loop, paid out as he makes his way higher. Lifted almost above the horizon, his head is in the clouds. But the figure that dominates the image, extending beyond clouds and city and river below, is that mineral black cable. It sustains the worker, it came before him, its elements will outlast him, its strength frees him (like Icarus) to climb high. The image would be coy if it weren't for the ambiguous blend of joy and strain on the skyboy's face, as if the exhilaration of defying earth's pull and rising into the Ariel element also exhausts the will.

Hine worked nearly as hard as his subjects. He lugged a bulky view camera and tripod and walked those girders. Because he wasn't a studio artist, he seems more a laborer than does a painter, sculptor, or writer. And among these, it's writers who don't act on or refigure matter; they don't produce material goods, at least not until the actual work is done, at which point another work process reifies the work into a book. Arendt says of poetry that it's "perhaps the most human and the least worldly of the arts, the one in which the end product remains closest to the thought that inspired it." She's mostly concerned with the objectification of work, and poets for Arendt are makers because their works are "thought things." Because of the thing-character of a poem, poets can be said to use "the same workmanship which, through the primordial instrument of human hands, builds the other durable things of the human artifice." This accounts for the object-laden quality of composition, and for the weighted, tactile sense poets have of their work, that writing is a thing-making labor. But it slights the thought-character of poetry, the intense immateriality of composition.

Imaginative writing rides close to the involuntary phantasmagoria of dreams and the worldless attention of a child at serious play. It's a contending of non-things—thought pressing against the imagination's emanations—and this process resolves into the "thought thing" of poetry. But poets want their work to have a certain fastness in the world, a physical presence. The more the work of poetry is patronized and presumed innocuous, the more poets protest that they really do work, that a poem has a made or fabricated character. Writers like too much to quote Yeats's "Adam's Curse"—"A line will take us hours maybe; / Yet if it does not seem a moment's thought, / Our stitching and unstitching has been naught"— as a statement of a poet's work, that the work *justifies* the activity. But it's also defensive, because Yeats knows that no matter how hard a poet works, harder than scullery maid or old pauper breaking stones, he or she will still be thought "an idler by the noisy set / Of bankers, schoolmasters, and clergymen / The martyrs call the world." Even if poets describe their work in terms such people might understand—as tedious, time-consuming cottage industry, knit-craft—they can't dislodge stubborn assumptions.

Most of us would like poems to be regarded as things, as essential facts, because it would pull poetry farther into the thing-world, make it a distinctive impinging piece of reality, which takes on a certain urgency in a civilization flooded with anonymous "products," media apparitions, and infinite replications. A great many people assume that the work of the poet is not to make a thing of beauty but to produce a beautifully functioning thing. No civilization has been so made of like products, and none has articulated its powers so massively by means of machines. Eugenio Montale and William Carlos Williams both called a poem "a little machine." The organic, associationist models of nineteenth-century poetics at some point gave way to an industrial model; by the second half of the twentieth century poets were talking about "torque" and "linchpins" and "scale" in "well-tooled" poems, and too many poets talk about "dismantling" or "repairing" their poems. The poet's work, in other words, is much closer to *techne,* to tradecraft or a work operation. Poetry is neither diminished nor debased by the mechanical model—though it *is* debased by the inauthenticity and professionalism the model encourages—so long as it doesn't surrender its complex and elusive thought-character.

Poets are driven to explanations and definitions of what they do because poetry can only be described, finally, in its own terms, but its terms are those of the imagination. In order to make comprehensible statements, we resort to analogue. The other arts have not borrowed so much from poetry's technical vocabulary as poetry has looted theirs. It's in fact the *search* for analogue, the irrational movements of attention and selection by which a poet discovers correspondences, which is more illustrative of a poet's actual work. But how to tell or picture that movement? (It's *like* trying to describe the forms that stir in a choreographer's thought as she shapes a new dance.) And besides, the writing of poetry really *is* work: it's physically and emotionally draining; it requires time, not only in the writing (which can happen fast) but in the discipline of preparation, of "framing"; and it may affect another person's existence. To believe poetry's task is to reply to living in a world of things, and that the poet's work is to receive the object world, can induce a sustaining fluency, at least for a while. It sustained Rilke through the composition of *New Poems (1907–1908)*, but in the silent period that followed he looked back on that productive time, writing to Lou-Andreas Salome in December 1911: "I expected nothing and no one and more and more the whole world streamed toward me merely as a task and I replied clearly and surely with work." On these conditions the work of poetry can respond powerfully to existence. But the conditions are narrow and dependent on the world's presentations, its object-occasions. If you remain too settled in the belief that poetry is a way of working the world's occasions, poetry will repose in asking habitual (or friendly) questions of the world; or it will become all sheeted, adversarial resistance to it—it becomes an argumentative response to life.

I know the adversarial position because it has sometimes, for good or not so good, kept me going. Coming from a culture of working-class southern European Catholics, I was bred to believe that work is, in conscience and in fact, the curse of the fall from grace, and that the curse determines and defines one's life. Adam brought himself down, bound himself to earth, and existence is the struggle to rise from the earth of work that compacts life in habit. Even if you were able to choose your work or trade, you never assumed it would be pleasurable. If you find work you like, you're lucky— luck, that little deity—but don't expect more. And yet, obligatory and maledicted as work was, not to work was sinful, scandalous, and only the holy idiot or gangster was exempt from its pains. The conviction that the work of poetry, though chosen (and by most measures unnecessary), is an adversarial engagement with the world, and that the task of writing is a life-sustaining answer, however muted, to that world, had its roots for me in religious belief and a very localized culture. Work was the way of suffering redemption. But this conviction turns the work of writing into a chastisement that shrivels the imagination. As a child I could read the gravities of work in the men I watched. They lived in what I think of as Caliban's world, what William James called "that distributed and strungalong and flowing sort of reality which we finite beings swim in." It's where the actual writing gets done. But some idealizing instinct let me see them also as arrangements of energy, each with its aura. Reviewing their working day, it was instinct in me to infuse their weightedness with some ethereal element. Lightened, lifted, they could be stopped and held in mind. The bricklayer on his scaffold is reshaping the sky. The iceman sails from the high black cab of his truck. My childish fancy was answering a real need, to rescue what I saw from the seductive life of habit, to see in work a lightness or upwarding. That instinct turned out to be work's most important element. It was Ariel's eager voice asking her magician-master: "Is there more toil?"

MAKE ME A PICTURE

I'm sitting on a small patch of sickly grass in the backyard of an aunt who lived in North Philadelphia. The endlessness of the blue sky, the scratchy ground, the tickly abrasive autumn air—I remember all that. I'm a toddler, bundled in a puffy snowsuit, chromium blue and crinkled, unlike the sky, whose wrinkle-free blueness is terrifically far. But I don't remember this as an actual experience. The subjectivity I feel for it—primal, alive in my skin, as real as that snowsuit and as unreal as that sky—comes from a photograph. There I am, on a small patch of backyard grass in a photo album my parents kept, long gone like them. It's a black-and-white image. How can the suit be blue? So much of life is camera-bound. I've come to believe, by some molecular pressure in my psyche, that my father took the picture. He loved making snapshots with his Brownie. He died when I was a teenager, and in one of the few mental images I have of him he leans over his little picture-making box, cupping the viewfinder to curb glare and squinting—even in fall's dimmest outdoor light he squinted as if on a sunny summer beach—down through it at me.

In "Portrait of Toddler in Backyard" I'm squinting in the autumn light, as I still do as a middle-aged man even on overcast days, my father and me looking for something in our squinty way, as if all actions were happening at once: pose, exposure, print, album setting, these words. I long ago internalized the photo as mortar in the construction site of self. It testifies to the reality of a childhood, to a subjectivity bulked out into space and time. But the fact is, I'm not even sure the photo existed: the image I have in mind may have developed as the kind of composite that neural networks create when we remember an image. I play with the notion that the photo was responsible for bringing me into existence. We sometimes sense a momentary resolution or dissolution of self in images. We come into being, or fade from it, in a picture. Or the ghost in the meat is taken hostage. (The Sioux called the camera a "shadow-catcher.") Any image will serve: a movie still, an album photo, a hyperventilated TV moment. It can catch us when we're vulnerable and dynamite the station of subjectivity where we negotiate the separation of inner and outer.

A photo portrait isn't as much an act of finding as a painting is. In painting, we sense the hand probing an imitation of what's given, the entire process rattled by the artist's feeling. Photographs are evidentiary but possess an insinuating, queasy-making mystery. Certain good ones propose conditions in extremis. In one of Duane Michals's pictures of Joseph Cornell, the figure (so stark, he's hardly there) stands before a mirror with no reflection, half his profile scraped away by light blasting through a window behind him. As a child, the first time I watched someone peel the glossy paper from a Polaroid-Land shadow-catcher and saw an image swoon into form, it was like witnessing an originating act, a technological genesis myth, something truly and entirely our modern own. There we are, my family and I: instead of ants or children emerging from a hole in the earth or sky, we're vapors materializing into dimensioned tints, forms just this side of vagueness, unstable, a little muddled, a little mortal. As for "Portrait of Toddler in Backyard" by Joseph Di Piero, I haven't seen it for at least forty years, if I ever did see it.

It's all one mirror, that barren backyard containing me and my snowsuit. Looking into it, I see myself looking into it, now, me being a history (or pileup) of images. What do I look like? I look like: (1) the unshaven petty thief in a T-shirt laminated on my driver's license; (2) the moody brooder on a book's dust jacket with plummy-shadowed, sanded-down skin; (3) the dopey-eyed, smirking Dago with pocked cheeks wearing a black leather coat, "exiting an unidentified Thai restaurant somewhere in San Francisco"; and (4) the tubby toddler in a gray snowsuit turning in the developer to icy, crinkled blue beneath a cream-into-azure ether. Our mirrors are absolutists of the real that can't be trusted. They make such a perfect simulacrum of life that they drain life from us. They curtail the hide-and-seek encounters that primitive mirrors of polished metal offered, where the reality of physical being depended as much on spiritual conviction. In a museum, in a Mayan mirror of polished iron ores (plated of tesserae to resemble a turtle's shell) I'm looking to find the proximate image of myself. The Maya believed mirrors had potent mojo and could divine the future. A mirror buried with a king was a safe conduct to rebirth. This particular stone seems haunted by my head. It's easier to believe in this image than the one the few mirrors in my apartment flash at me. I own a saucer-size shaving mirror and two wall mirrors much smaller than the framed photos of Bologna (by Ben E. Watkins) that hang near them. I don't want to catch glimpses of myself walking past. I don't want to haunt myself. I like to feel, not see, myself coming and going.

What do we expect of portraits? To be alarmed by a hard-angled strangeness, by the recognition that a painting or photograph makes manifest, or makes a secret of, things felt. We see what we want or need to see. Likeness is a slick vagrant. The dust jacket photographer printed a half dozen images from the ten rolls she exposed during our session. Our preferences parted ways. She liked the one with chin resting on clasped hands. I look so distinguished, I'm a personage, a multilingual world traveler who grew up listening to opera, studying art history, cultivating tomatoes with his adoring *mamma* in their backyard. Do you know where and how I grew up? I ask. Do you know about South Philadelphia working-class immigrant neighborhoods in the 1950s? I'm not exactly your Philippe de Montebello type. I know where and how you grew up, she says, but you *are* this anyway. And besides, I love that vein (which cables, Bela Lugosi-ishly, forefinger to wrist). She's looking at a picture. I, who look at pictures for a living, am looking for a semblance of self, of what I'd like to think I am. She's preoccupied with formal values. I just want a picture that looks like me, as if I knew what I really look like.

A good portrait is an investigation into possibility. It can make us feel realer than real or like a ghost of the flesh. We save photos of ourselves as ex-votos, tokens of thanks for being alive. Because portrait painting (or drawing) occupies significant durations of time, takes up time the way we take up space, feeling its way along, it's a more meditative activity than photography, which *practices* time. A photo depicts mortality, a painted picture represents it. A painting's aura seals in nonlikeness, floats it in the medium of pigment. A painted portrait makes a shape of the subject's inner life, a shape opaquely layered as an object of knowledge mediated by the artist's hand, a reality now more complex—or more simplified and irreducible—than it was before. For all their visceral intensity, photographs (black and whites, anyway) *are* auras, emanations, spooks: the sharpest photo can be more evasive in its delivery of the human form than the loosest painting or drawing. It's a token of lost time. Paintings aren't tokens, they're alternative presences of what's now real.

Not long ago, while sitting on that patch of grass in a backyard, I was sitting in the Upper West Side studio of the painter Paul Resika. We've known each other nearly twenty years. I've seen a great many of his paintings and he has read my books. He'd been wanting to paint me, but since I didn't have days to give up for an oil portrait, we spent a long afternoon talking, smoking cigarillos, and drinking sherry—very Philippe de Montebello— while he drew. An hour or so along I was confiding secrets (which is not my habit) and relating long-ago events that hadn't before snagged in my consciousness. I monologued (also not my habit), I couldn't shut up, I was being a real *chiacchierone,* as my family would say, wagging their hands as if flicking water from their fingertips. Roy Eldridge boiled from the CD player while I related an anecdote from my childhood, about a time when I briefly and uselessly took music lessons. "You should write about that," Resika said. And a year later, I do, but in the writing the originating anecdote turns into an essay on how in my youth music became inseparable from physical pain. It's pure self-portraiture. (But what is its truth?) Meanwhile, it's three hours later and Paolo has finished two drawings, one a suave, light-handed, rather fair likeness. "Not bad, this one," he says. "But I think I got something here." What he got was a portrait that snapped and roared at me—an angular, anxious head that looked not so much drawn as *struck.* He had found, or reimagined, animal quickenings in my inner life which only I (I thought) was aware of; the image also coined a sensation very familiar to me, a crude blending of idiotic irrational joy and fevered fear of living in a world of harm.

■

Good portraiture is an archive of invisible life, the subject's and the artist's. If you're the subject, chances are the portrait will be the really you in the not-so-likeness-of-you. An artist's language, if fresh and grasping, uses any available likeness to construe the artist's own temperament and feeling for reality. Resika's drawing flashed the excitability and expansiveness visible in his paintings, high-keyed colorist blasts gestured into recognizable motifs. Schiele made the body—no matter the identity of the sitter—a site for self-devouring, a machine of self-torture. In any Giacometti portrait, the head—a mass of scar tissue left as a record of the artist's exertions—is a planet of pentimenti. Kokoschka, who in a childhood accident fell into a maggoty pig carcass, made the human face a comic theater of lumpy exquisite disgust. The greatest diarist of selfhood was Rembrandt. In a self-portrait etched when he was forty-two, he sits at a table making an etching, looking out at his mirror, making the marks that are himself. It documents change and the very act of self-scrutiny. Toward the erosions and failings of old age, his own included, he showed a pitiless love. In an etching of his aged mother, the figure is locked into a contemplative pose, hand clenched on her breast, and we feel her entire body doing the work of final reflection—her flesh is a fatigued soul. The greatest living painter of agedness is Lucian Freud, for whom self-portraiture is an occasion to meditate on the mystery of incarnated consciousness. In his latest pictures, where the handling is freer than ever and driven by raw feeling, he makes flesh a dry, drab garment worn by a toughened but nearly depleted spirit. Head, eyes, and face have been lived into. Contingency has worked them over.

A year later, on another visit to Paul's studio, we're both shirtless, trying to keep cool in New York's gummy August heat. He's in his seventies, I'm pushing sixty. Our bodies don't want more gravity but it wants us, a story that's modeled in our sagging, wrinkled bodies. I'm telling him about a recently discovered cave in the Dordogne covered with engravings and drawings dating back twenty-eight thousand years. In addition to the usual bison and rhinos are drawings of naked human figures. Unusual for a Paleolithic cave site, there are also buried skeletons. Our earliest instinct was to represent what we thought we looked like, right there with the animals. The original making of marks wasn't just embedded in animist rituals, it was an impulse to give form to sexual embodiment—a few of the cave figures seem engaged in sexual display or activity—spoken in the same sentence as death and burial. I see that Paul has pinned the better of those two drawings to the wall. I want it for myself. I want to hang it near a mirror in my apartment. There he is, an "it," some "me" or other, stuck with messy internal goings-on, squirming on the studio wall, a nearly sixty-year-old man carrying more anger than is healthy, his poultry neck and newly dewlapped waist artfully concealed in a blousy blue snowsuit.

FORCE

In the autumn of 1995 I fell into despair. How else to say it? The constellated symptoms were those of disabling clinical depression, but no etiology can really accommodate the dimensions of the failure of hope. Hope not as a mood but as a casual existential assumption of life's continuity that lives in the spirit like involuntary reflex, like breathing. It wasn't my first time and wouldn't be the last. Anybody who falls once has usually fallen before and will sometime fall again. The circumstances aren't important any more, only the recognition that the despair stopped the ordinary circulatory motion of life in me and the physical world around me. Every soul experiences the death of hope in its own way. The wire can be tripped by the most trivial occurrence. I can't find a pencil, someone's line is busy, I burn the shirt I'm ironing, no mail comes. The gashing pain that ensues is so out of scale to its occasioning event that the pain can seem operatically silly. All the casual manipulations by which we cinch and stabilize our daily lives melt away into a formless, quivering, all-covering woundedness and frailty. I didn't wish it on myself and never thought what a dandy subject for poetry it might be. I wanted to be rid of it or it to be rid of me, and the longer it lasted the more it was like an evil-smelling visitor to whom I owed some inexplicable obligation of hospitality.

Despair is oblivion that doesn't set you free. If I hadn't been so oblivious, I might have remembered Gerard Manley Hopkins's bitterest lines, in one of the "dark sonnets" of 1885, where the best counsel he can give his despairing self is cheapie cliché: "Here! creep, / Wretch, under a comfort

serves in a whirlwind: all / Life death doth end and each day dies with sleep."
He knew the emotional and intellectual humiliation of having to cling to a
commonplace; that as the world turns we reach the edge of night and wait
for a new day. For a poet, whose personal and civic duty is to identify and
contest truisms, the consolation of cliché and nostrum can only make the
heart sicker, drier. And anyway, despair's fleeciness so suffocates the soul
that it kills any rescuing sentence. In my hell, I couldn't think of poetry, of
statements made in poems, because the pain ate up everything that came
near it, even my happy heckler, the offstage voice in my head primed to
mock my somberest tones and most self-important feelings. I just dropped
in to see what condition my condition was in.

Though now I think it might have helped to remember my Hopkins,
I also know that I'm not the sort of poet who reads poetry for solace or
who draws significance from poems because certain events and instances
in my life are fastened to them. I've never been a poetry lover, because
poetry hasn't been for me exclusively an object of consciousness. It's too
absorbed into the neediness, crude appetite, messes, and ambitions of my
subjective life. All the more reason, when writing, to deploy all that insti-
gating disorder in certain forms—forms that are autochthonous in that they
seem generated by nothing more than their own rough origins. The imaginative dimension a poem creates in language is like space in a painting, a
one-time event, a unique locale in which poetry (or image-making activity)
can happen. Poetry's space is composed and energized by formal dynamics.
I'm not talking about rhyme and meter. Form is a poem's internal economy,
the pattern composed of musicality, rhythm, and sense, created by whatever means. If, as the maxim goes, poetry teaches me how to live, it does
so in its mysterious effects of completed form. If it teaches, it does so by
shooting its formal force straight into the bloodstream of my consciousness, and it lives its life in me more as instinct than as moral awareness.
So it's not what's said in poems that has been exemplary to me, it's poetry's charged, whole, instantaneous pattern of form that is simultaneously
a pattern of feeling. I've never turned to it for healing or consolation. (If
I wanted that, I'd turn to religion.) Hopkins is exemplary because while
he recognizes the desperate need for the refuge of wise statements, that
recognition is composed into a pattern of speech which destabilizes the tidy
closure of received wisdom. The poetry I still most like to read, and which
shaped me when I was younger, is the kind that disrupts canny formulations

of the good life, and in its formal exertions probes and picks at the authority of its own inherited traditions. A poetry of moral niceties and Aristotelian assurances doesn't interest me.

And yet. In that bad time in 1995 I did turn to poetry, though I didn't know why. I now think I must have been reaching for some embodiment of possibility, or of hope, a pattern of hope. I paged through my old doughy paperback of Hart Crane and found this:

> The mind is brushed by sparrow wings;
> Numbers, rebuffed by asphalt, crowd
> The margins of the day, accent the curbs,
> Convoying divers dawns on every corner
> To druggist, barber, and tobacconist,
> Until the graduate opacities of evening
> Take them away as suddenly to somewhere
> Virginal perhaps, less fragmentary, cool.

These lines were enough to stir me from my depressive stupor and get me moving. I went out walking that night down Seventeenth Street through the Castro, then into the Mission, back up Market and my hill, a fifty-year-old man, stopping for coffee along the way so that I could read more Crane. Of the streets I remember only a large woman in mashed clothes shuffling along Market wearing fluffy oversized Bugs Bunny mules. The image of her heckled my momentous feeling that I was reading Crane as if my life depended on it, though my life did depend on it.

The despair of depression is a leaden, unrelieved immediacy that drains life of its ordinary, thrilling immediacies. It also obscures what Oliver Sacks and others say is an irreducible element in our makeup: a sense of style. Depression, which is totalitarian, crushes style and our feeling for it, style as a set of formal instincts and pleasures. A line of verse no more has to make an important statement than a picture has to depict a shared recognizable object. The way the tune falls, the feeling of a disorder at once expressed and momentarily stayed, a graspable shape of despair—these suffice. Those lines, from "For the Marriage of Faustus and Helen," like "Immemorially the window, the half-covered chair, / Ask nothing but this sheath of pallid air" from "The Harbor Dawn," and from "Voyages": "Meticulous, past midnight in clear time, / Infrangible and lonely, smooth as though cast / Together in some merciless white blade—— / The bay estuaries fleck the hard sky limits"—they delivered me from despair. Not by rational, deliberative process. It was more like electroshock, a saving jolt. I understand now that in my extremity a surge is what I needed. I've always more or less believed that poetry woos extremes in order to measure them into words. Crane was a special case in my life. Candied, visionary, overreaching Crane for good or ill was the first voice I really heard when I was young, and his dense, shining measures were the first measure I had of the possibilities of poetry. (I might have been better off having Dryden or Dr. Johnson as my first models, but that's not how it played out.) I still read Crane every few years, aware that when I was nineteen and living in that bricky walled city of South Philadelphia but sensing a world elsewhere, Crane's verse felt somehow like a promise of deliverance. Rereading him, he changes on me the way Keats, Yeats, Williams, and Stevens change (and as Hardy, Pound, and Frost do not). Several years ago I could hardly stand to hear his voice; he sounded like a Made-in-USA metaphysical or second-tier symbolist. I'm put off, though, by the same qualities that in other times claim me: the sentences that nearly break up from their own unrelieved metrical energy; the vatic assertiveness; the deflected public intimacies about sexuality; the intense, almost obliterating self-consciousness. In my despair, the poetry gave me yet something else: it balanced the painful grotesque voluminousness of hopelessness, a balance achieved by gorgeous extremities of formal feeling.

What delivered me was the way of saying something, not the something said. A poem's anecdote can satisfy certain of our emotional and intellectual needs because it creates a useful moral alignment or rightness. Crane's gift was to articulate feeling not by skeining statements around the armature of anecdote but by dissolving anecdote into the very muscle tissue of the verses. Those lines that helped me were meaningful not for what they said but for how they moved—poetry as animal presence. If I'd wanted the comfort of something said (which is one of poetry's powers, I don't deny this), I'd have turned to Frost and his ambiguous certainties, or to Philip Larkin's sour worldly wisdom. I'm speaking not only as a reader. The tiding cadences, the contractions and loosenings of texture, the excitements of consciousness lived out right there at the nerve ends of syllables—these have always mattered more to me than the sort of discursive poetry that tells us first one perceptive thing and then tells us another and another. A poetry displaying suburban ease and self-assured panache has its uses and pleasures, but it's not for me. I want a compound of words that turns strangely into something at once remote and insidious, completed and volatile. What delivered me momentarily from my bad time was the sheer force of form.

Crane is a conspicuous case of a poet who creates an idiosyncratic space in which poetry can occur, a space composed of formal dynamics saturated with feeling. The formal principles that let a poem cohere are not vehicles or enablers or transmitters of feeling, they *are* feeling. A poetry of statements can have this kind of force. Stevens's lines, "The poem is the cry of its occasion, / Part of the res itself and not about it," are a passion, not an illustration or depiction of a passion. I think it's not so crucial to have a signature manner as it is to have a signature form feeling. Then just about any line or stanza or phrase will enact in miniature the weave of the entire poem, and it frees a poet into changing ways of writing. Such freedom can lead, as the mannerisms of plain-style discursiveness cannot, to the borderland where the unconscious squawks through the finer tones of consciousness.

Crane's saving archangelical swoop was an unexpected gift. But grace in a time of emergency dims a little in the light of other bestowals. I soon realized that the shot his work had given me during my black-dog night was really just a momentary stay against more of the same kind of chaos. For several months I tried to give some sustainable balance to my inner life. After my spirit was punched awake, however, it lingered just this side of an opaque scrim behind which all physical reality seemed already dead or in the process of dying. I felt I'd been delivered from something awful to something merely less awful. The task of sanity was to bring myself to a brighter, more iridescent awareness, then to maintain it and, if I got lucky, intensify it. Inner coherence was what I needed and wanted, but for the work I do it had to be a coherence shaken by its own practice and fed by trouble.

I found an exemplary practice of this kind at the big 1996 Cézanne retrospective in Philadelphia. I didn't realize until then just how much I needed a demonstration of work empowered by its own changefulness and by its will to explore formal possibilities. Crane's firecracker was the right thing in its moment, but I felt I needed skills that would let me deliver myself. Cézanne's life of work, arranged so that at one point in the galleries it was possible to view panoptically a forty-year history of form-making instincts, is the evidence of an artist who lived so deeply inside himself that the activity of painting was itself the practice of the inner life. It was also an exercise of ongoing self-deliverance.

Crane and he were such different artists. Crane had so little time to change and develop, and when he killed himself it was as if the intensities he articulated in poetic forms finally overcame him. His leap from a ship, partly out of fear for his diminishing powers, is a bleakly apt image of the articulated self surrendering to the enveloping indefiniteness of the sea. Cézanne worked through and survived enormous youthful anxieties to build a mature, exacting art and a master style whose mechanics frequently challenged mastery of any kind. In contrast to Crane's flaring, damaged genius, Cézanne found, after much toil, a formal steadiness that enabled him to respond to the slightest sensation and to make that very responsiveness a vision of the physical world.

The great style grew awkwardly and pugnaciously out of the turbulence of Cézanne's early work. In the 1860s and 1870s he struggled to wrestle down into adequate forms his profound instabilities and dreads. His hot, riveting images of debauchery, rape, murder, and dissolution of all kinds are the work of an artist painting out of personal chaos, of flagrantly disordered feeling for flesh and nature. The portraits of the mid-1860s, made mostly with the palette knife, dramatize his attempt to master technique and therefore also master intensity. The stumpy, shingled loads of pigment are agonized exertions to make an adequate image of his feeling for life and form. His mature poetics are grounded in these early attempts to build images consistently out of discontinuities, wholeness out of broken surfaces. In the late 1870s, "Cézanne" begins to emerge: the painter of still lifes that inflect our perception of them even as they inflect their own structure and volume; of portraits which, as Karen Wilkin says, absorb into their diffident compositions the extreme unease Cézanne felt among people; of the resolute, momentarily becalmed presence of Mont Sainte-Victoire; and of bathers, the motif that freed him to express with sumptuous, spare clarity his feeling for the figure that flesh makes. The heated, anxious painter makes himself into an artist of rock-solid grace, nothing if not steady, a dog that every day gnaws on the bone of work. Cézanne identified with the hero of Balzac's story *The Unknown Masterpiece*, in which the painter Frenhofer, the greatest and most mysterious artist of his time, shows the young Poussin the unseen masterpiece he's been working on for many reclusive years. But when he calls Poussin's eye to the inventive drawing of a cheek or a back, the subtle execution of this or that passage, the young painter can see only a foot barely emerging from irresolute, unimaged chaos. Failing to see the just, impassioned forms, Frenhofer imagines a reality that doesn't exist.

Cézanne risked seeing his own ambitions vaporize if he could not find the formal inventions to enact them. The achievement of that, of completing feeling before it self-destructs or decomposes from its own vehemence, is itself exemplary—to make things like the *Large Bathers* of 1894–1905 that enact, not depict, the inner life, and to do so without having self-important designs on the audience. The figures in that picture—it's in the Philadelphia Museum of Art—are in process of coming into flesh while also streaming from and back into the landscape that contains them. The formal dynamics are themselves a vision of existence. This imaginative activity has its twin in the work of poetry. That stanza from Stevens continues: "The poet speaks the poem as it is, // Not as it was: part of the reverberation / Of a windy night as it is."

RIPE FRUIT

In the foreground of Bonnard's visionary 1926 picture *The Palm* stands a bourgeois housewife matrixed in wild vegetation like a primeval creature staring out at us, a piece of fruit in her hand. Each pictorial zone behind her isolates a discrete item: bridge, rural village, pastoral landscape (meadow, trees, farmhouse), body of water ridged by a cityscape. These serial scenes of the orders of nature and culture are gathered by a long palm branch that curves over them like a proscenium arch. The picture performs our emergence as creatures. *The Palm* isn't only Bonnard's vision of creation, it's a condensed natural history of his formal vocabulary. The village, with its pin-striped walls and roofs, has the decorative intimacy of the Vuillardesque interiors he made early in his career. The foliage has the vague, muted jubilance of the landscapes he painted around Le Cannet, the villa he bought in 1926 and where he spent much of his time until his death in 1947. The nebulous streaks of water are treated with the springy looseness that Bonnard possessed from the beginning, while the stiff spiny palm presides over that looseness like a watchful disciplinarian. And the woman, the Eve, has the knowing but diffident countenance we see in the many paintings he made of his wife Marthe. Eve faces out at us boldly and invitingly, with a bemused wakefulness Bonnard would investigate so intensely in the late self-portraits. She could be the meditative woman in Wallace Stevens's "Sunday Morning," questioning our imagination of Eden: "Is there no end of death in Paradise? / Does ripe fruit never fall?"

The Palm is a table of contents of Bonnard's career. At the beginning he seems already nearly fully formed. The head of a woman in a 1934 interior is fashioned out of the wallpaper behind her just as the heads of croquet players are rubbed forth from background foliage in a picture made forty years earlier. It's a commonplace that good painters arrive at looseness when they get old, as if loose handling were a kind of nursing home for forms. Cézanne's buoyant volumes and exposed canvas, Degas' monotypes, Matisse's cutouts. They didn't arrive at looseness, they worked naturally toward it. But Bonnard started loose, and to watch him pursue his vision over several decades of work is like watching the twitchy, glazing changes of a temperate climate. Unlike painters in whose company he belongs—Picasso, Braque, Matisse— Bonnard's mood and manner are steady. He didn't put himself through the aggressive self-remodeling and idiom changes that those others did. His evenness and apparent serenity mistakenly persuade us that he's the reliable painter prince of little pleasures. The familiar Bonnard, the one we think we're looking at, who constructed summery bucolic delights out of cobbled fields of pigment, who invented interiors at once aerated and hermetic, who in the great nudes of Marthe documented obsession and reserve, who made so many pictures possessing what Robert De Niro Sr. once called his "indolent, off-centered charm, more languorous than voluptuous"—this Bonnard is "Bonnard" *and* a disguised version of himself. If De Niro was right when, describing Bonnard's affinities with Watteau and Fragonard, he said that the pictures are "not about happiness, they *are* happiness," it's a conflicted happiness, complexly and at times disturbingly articulated, never a pure tone.

He can be chillingly melancholic about sensuous experience. In the great early picture *Man and Woman* a naked post-lovemaking male and female are walled off from each other by a bedroom screen that cleaves the picture. They're both turned away, paying attention to other things. She's in bed playing with her cats, he's washing, and the thick edge of the screen rises between them. Color narrates the estrangement. She's boxed in by a green margin that dips and circuits around her half of the picture and then creates the monumental screen. The florid red wallpaper behind her changes, on the man's side, to gloomy crimson wainscoting. It's a picture of intimacy as isolation and distraction. Bonnard was from the start skeptical of the pleasures of erotic relatedness. His 1907 painting of a faun shows a shaggy-rumped sexual marauder licking the neck of a panicked nymph. (It's so illustrational that it makes you want to kill content.) This blunt image of ecstatic predation gets transformed in the later work into a constant watchfulness of the dissolutions involved in sensual experience. Watching Bonnard's wrist make marks, following him as he constructs the something seen as an idiosyncratic way of seeing it, we're watching the surges, hesitancies, doubts, anticipations, and withdrawals of erotic melancholy. Composition seems not fused to a structure but floating on it. The technique of *Man and Woman* acts out his desire to achieve both the motion of memory—the extravagant movements by which we reimagine sensory experience—and the stilled instant fixed in an image.

Bonnard described painting as "the transcription of the adventures of the optic nerve," and he works at that by means of thousands of islanded marks and separations. In nearly every mature painting we can see the construction of color, sometimes hot and sluggish, sometimes cool and choppy. He wants us to see at the same time the process of the proliferation of marks by which a painting comes into existence and the structure that holds those fluid increments together. So many of the pictures enact little agonies of pleasure plied in unstable tremulous surfaces, pooled or pebbled colors, optical distortions, and the bleeding through of hues and objects. In a sumptuous late picture, *After the Meal,* the eye falls first upon a bowl of fruit at the center of the scene, then follows yellow and red traceries that pounce from the bowl to define the sweater of a woman clearing the table, then the table legs, the mantel in the background, and finally the stiff figure of a second woman coffined in a door frame and about to enter the room. That apparitional, distorted figure (she's pygmied) is the last thing the eye catches. The painting is stately and fantastical, articulated and mizzled, and the off-to-the-side figure—Bonnard's pictures are full of isolation booths: windows, mirrors, doorways, bathtubs, picture frames—occurs to the eye the way certain dream figures do, when we know we're in a dreadfully familiar place about to be violated by an intruder we sense only at the rainy edge of consciousness. That figure, the woman leaning over the table, the fruit, the serving plate, the bottles of wine and water, are all built up into a methodical, meticulous looseness so massive and dense that both image and handling are saturated with a feeling of unsatisfied appetite, unmet desire.

Bonnard's gorgeous vernal palette is muted by recognitions that give the work a casual pensiveness. We see it in the turn of Marthe's head. Over the many years she posed for her husband, her complete face is shown only a few times. Usually she's looking down, turning away, or shying from a mirror. If the body is the face of character, Marthe's character is sensuously diffident. It's not that she's lost in reverie or in the attentions of the moment but that she's veiled by consciousness, not really possessed of it. The Marthe pictures, like the interiors, are a confidence. They confide in us a way of viewing physical reality desirously and the strategies by which one goes about representing that vision. The more forcefully and completely Bonnard presents the physical world to us, the more cunningly he withholds it. While giving us the atomized and agglomerated delights of material reality, he's also making us study the way we see: he makes us list toward the pictures wantingly. The mechanics of bounty and suspense are all one powerfully mixed tone. A big yellow nude from 1931 is a monumental image of concealment and deflectedness (her back is turned toward us, head turned to one side) worked out in explosively sheeted color. The washy, assertively tentative paint plays out Bonnard's deepest ambitions, to divulge while restraining, to expand while retaining, to make a picture a becalmed cry toward the wanted object. The pictures of Marthe in the cartouche of her tub have an almost smothering physical immediacy even while she seems aloof and inviolable, delivered from our gaze as she's delivered to it. She spreads (and begins to disintegrate) along the stippled skin of water laid on the plane of the tub, each surface—flesh, water, metal—embedded in and layered on the other. Marthe looks at first like a hedonist's offering, but this changes as we realize that in the life of the paint she's being called back from us. We're not allowed to forget that she's hostage to the painter's eye. The desirousness spiking into the pictures is deflected by the very means used to manifest it. This double action of boldness and obliquity can be unsettling, but the unsettledness is a complex pleasure.

Bonnard's execution makes a lot of Matisse look too thought out. Little disruptions of superb accident conduct us from passage to passage. I love a savage passage in the early *Nude with Green Slipper* where the midriff of a woman bending over to cream her legs buckles more than it should. The bright green slipper at the lower right, the first thing the eye picks up, and the figure's red face (turned down, of course) work together to direct our gaze to that crunched stomach. In the time it takes to gather and organize the picture's contents, Bonnard has changed the volume and space. Then there are pictures that look like they've been modeled from the inside out, arriving at a state somewhere between florid material reality and vaporization. Sublimely calm interiors, still lifes, gardens and landscapes which seem to be remembered from some primordial time when the natural order was all one fused plenitude (Bonnard let his garden at Le Cannet grow wild) distend and contract like the nudes, with a considered suddenness. Marthe's body always seems to be inhabited by a self-inquiring, form-giving will. In *The Bathroom* she arches her back in such a way that we feel the force of the painter's formal curiosity as an invisible hand pushing and lifting the small of her back. It's exhilarating when this sort of thing happens, though it's usually the not entirely pleasurable exhilaration of vertigo. The pitch of tabletops in some pictures is so steep, even while the objects on them are correctly placed, that it disorients and dizzies us. Bonnard isn't brainy and magisterial like Matisse, or martial and sly like Picasso, but he *is* delicately insidious in the way he determines how our eye half-perceives and half-invents reality, how we imagine we see a shared world. He once told a model that he wanted "presence and absence." I think he meant that he wanted memory lived out as shaped substance.

So much of Bonnard is about the flesh tending to its necessities and delights, in the ablutions of the bath, the provisioning of table settings, the views from window or terrace which become visions of a First Garden, that the self-portraits, especially the late ones, in their audacious close-up exposures of the body, exist as an enormous condition of Bonnard's vision of happiness. In *The Boxer*, the scrawny adult raising his fists looks like a helpless child quivering in authentic but slightly silly rage. In the severe self-portraits of the 1940s, he fills the canvas with human presence. There's no meliorating or redemptive surround. The picture space is the mirror in which he appears to himself. The image is pushed forward, as if spread upon the front of the canvas, as it would appear in a mirror. Now, finally, after so many pictures of Marthe tantalizingly looking away, we see a face fully exposed, confronting itself. In whatever guise or pose—an interrogation subject, a Chinese sage, a stiff professorial type, a bemused painter—he makes himself into *the* human being, the prototype Adam we would expect to see in a picture like *The Palm*. He recalls Lear's vision of unaccommodated man, and in one of his last paintings, *Self-Portrait in the Bathroom Mirror*, the frail, naked, skin-headed presence is Lear's "bare, fork'd creature," the shapely living flesh left unheroically to its own deteriorating form. (What's heroic is the *making* of these pictures.) Their ravishing intimacy lies in the recognition that we die as most of nature dies, but we die capable of representing ourselves to ourselves. They have a sublime tight grandeur, though the handling is looser than ever.

UNLOVELY UNLOVABLE

The only thing available to us is the reality of our dreams in images.
—Beckmann, Diary, 1946

All his working life, Max Beckmann read literature and philosophy, but I don't suppose he knew Hamlet's remark, "I could be bounded in a nutshell and count myself a king of infinite space—were it not that I have bad dreams." It fits Beckmann's enterprise. His art was never tentative or discreet, but it's rich with uncertainty and ambiguity. He articulated a century's historical realities with imagery trapped in garishly lit middle zones between nightmare and wakefulness. Whatever the subject—anecdote, portrait, still life, landscape, conversation piece—he charged it with event-consciousness. Picture-making wasn't just an art practice, it was spiritual record-keeping. (He kept other sorts of records, too: diaries, letters, essays, lectures.) The infinity of space terrified him. Nonillusionist pictorial space—nonce space—wasn't just a modern painterly problem, it was a physical reality that might have embedded or encoded in it a transcendent reality; it was, at the least, a medium for the desire for some kind of transcendence. Contracting depth and volume into two dimensions gave Beckmann momentary solace and equilibrium when confronting what he called "the great void and uncertainty of the space that I call God." ■

One can be new ... based on the old laws of art: plasticity in the plane.
—Letter, 1922

Art historical alignments are hard to dislodge. An article on Beckmann in the *New York Times* a few years ago called him an Expressionist. The same newspaper had called him the same thing in 1939. Beckmann detested Expressionism, calling it "a decorative and literary matter," an affectation that rushed into quasi-abstract forms—he had Nolde and Marc in mind—an emotionality unmediated by reason and by the deliberations of pictorial structure. He was consistent in his disapproval. He didn't like Gauguin and famously disliked Matisse because they painted "flat," screen-ish, and retreated from the big-boned, voluminous picture-making he aspired to. Beckmann's restlessness was certainly brawnier and more weighted by the experience of history. If you look at the early *Small Death Scene*, though, you understand the Expressionist claims. Several streaky, quivering figures gathered inside and outside a death room act out attitudes of grief: paralyzed reserve, shrieking sorrow, hysterical fatigue. In a picture like this, he's closer to Soutine and Kokoschka (though cannier and more diverse), who like him are penned up as Expressionists because there's nowhere else to put them. Beckmann began as a history painter with the oversized, ambitious 1912 picture *The Sinking of the Titanic*, modeled after Géricault's *Raft of the Medusa*. It's a specific anecdote rendered as world panic. Several lifeboats, boiling up through the picture space, pitch sickeningly in sight of the iceberg and ship that float high in the composition. Beckmann was twenty-eight at the time, and the picture's massive busyness is pure bravura—but the action, the churned-up pouches of anguished, despairing castaways, is merely stated, not poured into image-life. By contrast, another early, smaller canvas, *The Street*, which like *The Sinking of the Titanic* renders a particular place in time (Berlin, 1914), crams into a stage-set space a cluster of figures—poor woman, rich woman, young child, baby, Beckmann himself, horse and driver—with a formal explosiveness, rocky with local detonations, missing from the Titanic picture. ∎

Gauguin was not capable of extracting from our own time—murky and fragmented though it may be—types that might be for us, the people of the present, what the gods and heroes of past peoples were for them.
—"Thoughts on Timely and Untimely Art," 1912

Beckmann developed a set of types which played out the experience of history as terror: Adam and Eve, monarch and soldier, murderer and murdered, leader and lackey, torturer and victim, stage manager and actor, concierge and bellboy, ringmaster and clown, and the manipulated self— *his* in the self-portraits. Experience shaped his passion. In 1914 he enlisted as a medical orderly in the German army. He saw and ministered to many bad· things, and after a nervous breakdown in 1915 he was discharged. He became famous during the Weimar years and was considered by some the most important artist of his generation. When the Nazis came to power in 1933, he was fired from a teaching position in Frankfurt and soon his work, like so much modern art, was under attack by National Socialism. In 1937, living in Berlin, Beckmann was included in the regime's "Degenerate Art" exhibition. He'd already been anticipating the world trouble Hitler would make and so fled with his wife to Amsterdam (he never returned to Germany) and lived there until 1947, when he emigrated to America, first to St. Louis and then New York, where he died in 1950. Beckmann was a city man, born in Leipzig, trained in Frankfurt, spending frequent chunks of time in Paris—his idea of "the South" was Genoa: he made a stupendous, ominous nocturne of its harbor and train station—but it didn't entirely matter where he found himself. "In every city," he wrote in his 1947 diary, "I always hear the lions roar!" He never much cared for the company of artists, but he was especially isolated in Amsterdam, spending longer hours than usual in his studio, an old tobacco storeroom. He went from being a celebrity to someone the Dutch didn't want to know about. During these years he called his art a form of self-hypnosis, and the figures that populate his more bloodily discordant pictures do seem an induced rather than an invented phantasmagoria. He said many times that he wasn't a political man, but he had a signature vision of historical reality. His artistic heroes after World War I, when his figuration becomes hard-angled, and space seems a suffocating affliction invented by unfriendly gods, were Gothic masters of the suffering flesh like Grünewald, Gabriel Mäleskircher, and Brueghel.

The gaunt angularity of anatomy and scene in an early religious picture like *Descent from the Cross* puts a jackknifing pressure on the picture space, and the stiffness of mass becomes part of his expanding idiom. ■

My aim is to get hold of the magic of reality and to transfer this reality into painting—to make the invisible visible through reality . . . which forms the mystery of our existence.
—"On My Painting"

There's fog and bluster in Beckmann's reflections—he picked up bits of vocabulary from Nietzsche, Schopenhauer, and Hume—but there are real parallels between what he said and what he did. In "On My Painting" and other writings, he talks about the self as the object of our journey in life and art. The self is "the great veiled mystery of the world," and for this reason Beckmann pursued the idea of self-realization of "the so-called whole Individual" in his work. The self, as I understand it here, is the entity constructed from appearances and from the inner life, formed by experience, historical consciousness, self-awareness, and memory. It's the subject of the works I most admire, the self-portraits. In drawings he played with try-it-on identities. In 1911 he's Max the Mysterious, glaring out from a heavily cross-hatched black aura. "You are in my power," it says. (But you are not getting sleepy.) In 1921 he's a successful Thomas Mann–like bourgeois artist complete with bowler hat and mildly arrogant glance. In 1946 he's the complete artist, mature of physical form, wearing a beret, completely inside himself; the aging body houses awareness of the best and worst of human action. The painted self-portraits are even more responsive to inflections of self. In an early postwar picture of himself at the easel, wearing a red scarf, he has a strung-out, neurasthenic look, as if recording bad nerves directly onto the canvas he's leaning on for support. Like Bonnard, the southernest poet to this northerner, he costumes himself—as a sailor (with speedy, dashing effects), a swell in a tux (the paint very constructed), and (in the picture I'm craziest about) a carnivalesque figure in a wildly striped orange and black dressing gown, which might be mistaken for a commedia dell'arte costume, peeking and frowning from behind a brass horn. He's following the rules good artists live by: surprise art by surprising yourself; push back at what you know how to do; keep changing. That 1938 horn picture—it's in the Neue Galerie in New York—surprises with dashing flicked grace notes of color, racy passages, and underpainting that lets Beckmann build up unusually crusty surfaces with dusty tints. He's the artist as self-impersonator, the clarion-caller pausing before or after the blast, casing reality, looking suspiciously at *our* selves, a roustabout angel who brings us the best and worst news. ∎

I have tried to realize my conception of the world as intensely as possible.
—"On My Painting"

His cities roared at him, and he roared back in *The Night* (1918–19). A cluttered-attic interior bursts with a horrible, funhouse pileup of agonies. A burly mustachioed ruffian holds the woman he's abducting like a piece of stiff cardboard scenery. A barely visible peasant type is hanging a man from the rafters whose gaping mouth seems to be wailing a "why-are-you-doing-this" to such irrationality. A well-dressed barefoot clerk with a bandaged head twists the hanging man's arm while smoking a pipe. A nearly naked woman, the central figure, her back turned toward us, hands bound to a window, splays her legs helplessly. Her shape is all hopeless, deflated resistance and violability. Scholars offer allegorical readings of this picture and the later, more complicated triptychs, but I take Beckmann at his word when he says that many of his figures have a wobbling ambivalence filled out by viewers who should be guided in understanding, he said, "by their own inner light." My inner light makes this picture a comically horrific gang portrait of unreason. The awfulness and tortures are presented as simply things that happen to be happening. At the time, there was certainly sufficient grimness to go around. George Grosz and Otto Dix both responded to a comparable order of northern European experience during and after World War I, but they were satirists whose surgical instrument was the line. Beckmann's painting is a global criticism of life, not the local criticism of satire. What separates him from his equally worldly contemporaries (and from other major twentieth-century artists) is the hoarse bass drone of world sorrow throughout his work, even when the pictures squirm with horror-show high jinks. ∎

I try to capture the terrible, thrilling monster of life's vitality and to confine it, to beat it down and to strangle it with crystal-clear, razor-sharp lines and planes.
—"A Confession," 1918

One of my favorite paintings in the San Francisco Museum of Modern Art is Beckmann's 1938 *Woman at Her Toilette, with Red and White Irises*. A heavy-hipped woman in negligee bends over a vase of flowers, washing her hands. It's packed tight with specific excitements. The graceful but inexorable gravity of the woman's mass, bulked out with the classical rotundity Beckmann had mastered in beach pictures and nudes of the late 1920s, meets resistance from the blooming irises and other V-shapes repeated in the woman's fleshy arms, the space her arms craft, and her lingerie's skirt and off-the-shoulder straps. A plunging or rocketing spearhead or chevron is the elemental form in Beckmann's vocabulary. It appears as fish, plants, fingers, splayed legs, king's crown, ship bows, and daggers. It wedges momentous feeling into place. His most scabrous and outraged image of Nazi culture, *Hell of Birds*, done the same year as the iris painting, is a vicious ritualistic riot of beaks, wounds, talons (in Sieg Heil position), knives, and feathers that could double as knives. I don't know any other important modern artist who painted so often out of fury—for and at experience and meaning—or who was, picture by picture, so squarely uncharming. His formal aspirations were inseparable from his raucous visionary prowess. As a maker— colorist, draftsman, performer, personality—Beckmann had a feeling for what he believed had compelled great art since antiquity, the "mystery of being." His impudence was puggish and daunting. It was a different order of confrontation from the boldness of Braque and Roualt (whom he admired) and of Matisse and Picasso (whom he didn't). He was a classical personalist who, while the pictures are often a jagged weave of ambivalent imagery and uncertainty, showed no creative self-doubt. The images were a complete expression of the personality. Even when sardonic or baleful tones tense up a picture, the affect underlying and sustaining everything is that jangling sorrow, which gives his pictures their clarifying remorselessness. ■

The contemporary artist is the true creator of a world that did not exist before he gave shape to it.
—"The Artist in the State," 1927

As a young artist Beckmann aligned himself with the Neue Sachlichkeit, the New Objectivity that countered Expressionism's slurred forms and operatics. He wanted the reality of the picture to bear lucid feeling. He held to this even after he began making triptychs in 1932. He completed ten and left one unfinished at his death. They depict physical and spiritual worlds in collision, contemporary secular imagery—circus, theater, parlor—banging against baggy symbologies drawn from pagan, Christian, and kabbalistic traditions. Scholars give straight-up readings of them, but I'm easy with shiftiness. Beckmann was more interested in mystical insinuation than narrative; he loads stiff, hard-edge forms with supple suggestiveness. Each "symbol" is really a wobbly iridescence, taking on significance from its ambience and flashing forth a multiple suggestiveness of its own. Consider fish. In the right panel of *Departure,* in the Modern, two lovers bound upside down to each other compose a fishy form; a bellhop (who turns up in several pictures) offers them a stiff red fish before they fall in the water. In the center panel, a man, a royal redeemer of some kind, holds a net full of fish. In *The Argonauts* an ancient rises on a ladder from the sea, the source. Fish as sexual sign, Christian story, pagan myth. A fish is also, in its way, an *onderduiker,* a diver or submerger, the word applied to Jewish children hiding in cellars during the Nazi occupation of Holland, while Beckmann was in Amsterdam, children whose legs we see under the stage in the *Actors* triptych, the underground reality beneath the staged one, though at the same time the legs belong merely to extras waiting their cue. When asked, Beckmann either refused to apply meanings to specific images or else kicked up more dust. "The fish signified Christ," he once said. "I use it with its vapid stupid look—as a symbol of man's bewilderment at the mystery of eternity." I think Beckmann designed each triptych as a labyrinth of provocations. I get disoriented by their meandering insinuations and am satisfied *because* they don't cohere. Beckmann told a dealer that the perfect viewer of these congested pictures is someone whose inner life carries the same "code" as his does. He also said the pictures were never intended to be objects to decode. ■

It is not the subject that matters but the translation of the subject into the abstraction of the surface by means of painting.
—*"On My Painting"*

Two late pictures. A vanitas still life from 1945, with three skulls and playing cards. Jaunty skulls, grinning large, one biting down on the ace of spades. The space is crushed forward, so that all the merriment seems stood up on the tabletop, not presented to but *pushed at* us. Not the sort of carnivalesque gaiety we were expecting. The subject may not matter, but the translation of the subject is everything. And Beckmann's last self-portrait, from 1950. He's dressed in a royal blue jacket (a red chevron edges its sleeve), a wary, middle-aged student of the world. We see the skull under the skin but not the mouth, covered by a long thin hand pinching a cigarette, a gate (like the horn) between him and us. The handling is quick and gestural and frank, but the compositional entirety recedes from us, not shy or evasive but uneasy, leery. It's the only self-portrait that gives up a self-control we didn't know existed in the others until he made this one. He looks submerged in himself and lost to time. ■

OUR SWEATING SELVES

Years ago, while visiting Lanciano, the major city in the province of Abruzzo, I saw a reliquary in the Church of San Francesco containing an opaque brownish wafer that was said to be living tissue from the body of Christ. The priest in charge assured us that scientists have corroborated this "life." I was with my Abruzzese cousin, a pious, unquestioning man who whispered his awe to me explosively, as a child would. The priest, the kind of severe adult who would scold the child, was a sour man who spoke with pinched, impatient aloofness, as if he knew we could not possibly understand the significance of what he was showing us. He seemed to me someone who, having miserably suffered a crisis of faith, emerges with deepened belief that is inseparable from deepened disdain for nonbelievers. Like my cousin, I felt awe in the presence of the relic, but for different reasons. That slice of flesh—it looked like sepia-stained amber—was a token of the Incarnation, the most elusive, terrifying, and melancholy mystery of Catholicism. The hypostatic union is Christ's grandeur. As a child I was enthralled by the fact of the god in the flesh, the mortal able to bring himself back from the land of the dead. As an adult fallen from belief and still falling, I think more about the flesh of the god and our condition (as Hopkins says) of being bound to our bones, fastened to flesh.

When I read Dante's *Inferno* and *Purgatorio* I'm aware that it's the story of a body of a certain voluminous substance tracking its destiny among insubstantial *ombre*, shadows. Every time Dante realizes he's a solid object passing among those who are without solidity, aware of his own thingness (though he couldn't and wouldn't have thought of himself or any human being in these terms), the poem commemorates and celebrates the Incarnation. It's in imitation of Christ that Dante lives out the most acute, finely calibrated awareness of the body in premodern literature. In poetry he was giving the body an earthbound opacity and solidity that Giotto was giving it in painting. Following Virgil into Phlegyas's boat to cross the river Styx in Hell, he notices that only then does the boat seem *carca*—laden, weighted. Dante is following his powerful predecessor by imitating him: when Aeneas in Virgil's epic steps into the Stygian boat, it groans under his weight. But *carca* has shadow meanings: the boat, when this creature is in it, is fraught, *charged*, as we speak of being charged with a duty or task. In that place of shades, the boat is charged with the presence of flesh and blood, of memory embodied. Crossing the river, Dante notices how the prow cuts the water more deeply than when it carries others. That channel is the first mark of embodiment in the underworld, where souls who have no substance suffer real physical pain. It is human presence carving its record into Hell's topography.

Dante's inspirited heft assigns him a special position in the order of the universe. Beatrice later explains to him that all things have order among themselves, and it's this orderliness, this form, that makes the universe like God. The more responsive he is to the world's physicality, to its proper weights and measures, the more the poet participates in and contributes to godly order. His desire is physically expressed in the many kinds of seeing he does: he looks, stares, marvels, regards, peers. It's an act of piety for Dante to get things right, to present the consistency and stability of things in exact detail. To describe the degree of lightness of big fiery flakes falling on the heads of those who defied God, he says they fall "come di neve in alpe senza vento," "like windless mountain snow."

His walk through Hell is a series of recognitions of human wrongness, recognitions shaped by the different kinds of resistance his body meets. Once he breaks through the point of absolute gravity on Hell's floor and emerges in the light of day—true sunlight, not the travesties of light he saw in Hell—he delivers himself of his weightedness. Now it's the body-as-stuff that matters. When the shades in Ante-Purgatory approach him, anxious for memories received and transmitted, they pull back in shock because they see light on a rock broken by Dante's shadow. The moment is so compelling because it's as if Dante has *just now* acquired a shadow, just now given volume to define and articulate his fraughtness. He's the thing-that-throws-a-shadow. Virgil's words to the souls, "What you're seeing is a human body," make that fact seem strange and marvelous. Shade, his mortality print, becomes Dante's new companion in Purgatory, a memory trace of the sinfulness whose horrific consequences he witnessed in Hell among *le ombre*—the shades.

When the Hale-Bopp comet passed close to the earth in 1997, my memory of that Lanciano relic struck me with the kind of force that Dante describes when in Purgatory he first sees Matelda (the beautiful young woman who replaces Virgil as his guide) on the opposite bank of the river Lethe: it's "a thing of such wonder that it drives away every other thought." I'd never seen a comet, and now there it was, framed in my window night after night, a lumpy smear of ice and space dirt coinciding, in ways I felt but did not understand, with the reality of a tissue of live flesh two millennia old.

Such coincidence is often the occasion of poems. Crude, nebulously related material begins to take on a felt shape of meaning in consciousness. So of course I tried to write something, anything. But the more I wrote in answer to the occasion, the more inert and intractable that coincidence became. The two events existed in meaningful relation merely because they happened to occur to me, significant because they were the accidental conjunction of unrelated celestial and earthly facts. The bully of subjectivity was trying to muscle the material into a meaningful pattern, to will poetry into existence out of atomized haphazardness. I think many poets now live in a vague Emersonian world of spiritual becoming, without a justifying, sponsoring, divinely authored cosmology. "This one fact the world hates," Emerson says in "Self-Reliance," "that the soul *becomes;* for that forever degrades the past . . . confounds the saint with the rogue, shoves Jesus and Judas equally aside." I live with the conflicted belief that spirit or soul, a restless processual dynamic we live toward and into at the same time, is whatever consciousness conceives or imagines to be greater than itself. I think not so much about the soul's eternality as about its earthly self-definition.

My modest problem made me think of Dante's poem, in which celestial and earthly realities are a bonded pattern of correspondences, alignments, and coincidings authored in and by Divine Mind. Because he possesses "il ben dell'intelletto"—good mind, godly mind, virtuous consciousness—Dante perceives and instruments these relationships and dramatizes himself as part of that massive coherence. The *Comedy* and the universe it represents are beautifully rotund and complete. It's two hours before dawn on Easter Sunday in the year 1300 when Dante, under the morning star of Venus, arrives at the mount of Purgatory, the southern pole precisely opposite the northern pole of Jerusalem. The poem is authorized to contain earthly history, celestial events, and divine interventions in one ordered, balanced structure. Dante had agency (the pilgrim and his guides), purpose (the beatific vision), and process (education by bearing witness). He applied a mechanics of foreknowledge and remembrance by which everything that surprises us and Pilgrim Dante as he makes his way has already happened. The journey is complete before it commences, and is complete most of all when Dante seems most vulnerable to contingency, to the pressurized circumstances that squeeze us every moment. While we're reading it, the poem jumps with possibility and accident even while we hold in mind its finished, resolved structure. The poem is busily intimate—we're kept physically close to Dante and his humanness—and shockingly remote.

Many of us are the more or less deformed grandchildren of Thomas Hardy's sorrow that destiny is ruled by crass casualty, by accident and random coincidence, unreasonable, purposeless, unsponsored. Most of what I write is not only about contingency, it's grounded in it, in what Hopkins calls "our sweating selves." Hazard, whatever its consequences, is a species of beauty, but it's not rounded and self-enfolding, it's angular and fragmentarily expansive—Big Bang beauty. Lady Fortune, who has her own fixed place in Dante's cosmos, in this new scheme becomes a terrorist. According to the *Comedy*, the goddess's turning wheel determines change: the sudden loss or acquisition of wealth; political tumult or peace; the death or good health of a child. Unchanging in her changefulness, Lady Fortune oversees the orderliness of accident as a manifestation of divine plan. What we experience as terrifying uncertainty and irresoluteness exists by perfectly ordered divine dispensation and sponsorship. The *Inferno* and *Purgatorio* are theaters of fortune, where the process and consequences of change are in a constant state of motion, of excited reenactment and disclosure. But they're also display cases in which discrete actions are suspended and tableauxed in the larger order of the poem.

Dante's journey is discovery-through-instruction: he's destined to happen upon what he needs to know but doesn't expect to find. Having "chanced upon" his esteemed teacher Brunetto Latini or the haughty Florentine politico Farinata or La Pia, killed on her husband's orders, he's somehow changed because his understanding of divine order and the human place in it has been enlarged. The poem's cosmology justifies the trepidation, anxiety, and uncertainty he experiences. The more each witnessed event seems like chance, the more divinely ordered it must be. The poem offers us, whether we're believers or not, a fully articulated order that can account for the entire range of human experience, and a model of human consciousness that can imagine being indentured to chance *and* delivered eternally from it.

The *Comedy* is one of the most relentlessly subjective poems ever written, although it's not about subjectivity and certainly not about the kind of modern ironic selfhood that Shakespeare invents in Hamlet, Prince Hal, and Macbeth. In his great book *Dante: Poet of the Secular World*, Erich Auerbach says that even before the *Comedy,* in the *Vita Nuova*—the prose-and-verse book where he describes his first meeting with Beatrice and the pain it brought him—Dante intensified his feeling "by raising it above the sphere of subjectivity to which feeling is ordinarily confined by establishing it in the empyrean realm of the ultimate and absolute." Later poets didn't need an ultimate, eschatological plan in order to perceive the self as a unified entity. Sheer intuitive power, Auerbach says, enabled later writers to combine inner and outward observation into a whole. He sees the history of European literature as a fall into unredeemable contingency, into the recognition that human life turns on a series of accidents or uncontrollable events, only sometimes mediated (and even then vaguely or slightly) by supernatural agency. Knowledge of contingency is tragic knowledge.

Nothing happens by chance in the poem. Everything occurs in covenant with divine order. And yet the pilgrim's experience is dramatized in such an exquisitely seamless, humanized way that he experiences events as we do—he happens upon whatever happens. We experience with him the thrill and trembling of being a child of contingency. Ezra Pound said that a poet's duty is to make accurate reports. Dante says that he wants to relate events "sì che dal fatto il dir non sia diverso," "so that what I say is exactly how it was." Every encounter is coincidence, and he feels it to be so, but he knows—it's knowledge indistinguishable from feeling—that all coincidence is aligned and justified in the mind of God. This double knowledge accounts for what I've been trying to describe as the remote, exotic strangeness of the poem, and at the same time it accounts for the humane passion of Dante's imagination: every encounter where he's shown to be completely human is webbed into the unquestionable presence of God's plan. The poem is both an intimacy and a decree, the open field of a hermetic system.

Certain lines in the poem are talismans. I recall them when I'm distressed or anxious, or to protect me from writing badly, as if they could. In the Paolo and Francesca episode, when Dante describes cranes flying single file, singing their love songs, the sound weave, the songfulness of "E come i gru van cantando lor lai"—those droning *n*'s and elegiac "lor lai"—express before the fact the mournful pity Dante will feel toward the two lovers. One of my favorite tercets hums a tricky, accurate fact. It comes in the Master Adam canto when Virgil scolds Dante for staring too amazedly at the scene of Sinon (who deceived Troy into accepting the wooden horse) and the mandolin-shaped counterfeiter Master Adam punching and vilifying each other. Dante, wanting to excuse himself but unable to form the words, describes himself "like someone who dreams he's being hurt / and while dreaming, wishes he were dreaming: he desires / what's already happening as if it weren't." Be patient with me here. The Italian encodes something that is probably impossible to get in translation: "Qual è colui che suo danneggio *sogna*, / che sognando desidera sognare, / sì che quel ch'è, come non fosse, *agogna*." *Sogna / agogna* is an experiential rhyme: to dream / to desire. The language swoons and insinuates, and yet the lines have a cool, purposeful psychological precision. That word *agogna*, which my Dante dictionary defines as "to fervently desire" (*desiderare ardentemente*), bears so much of what makes us human but which, according to doctrine, must be directed by the will only toward the good: the line locks in a complex Thomistic dynamic.

And there's this. On Purgatory's second terrace Dante sees a congregation of the envious, their eyes stitched shut with wire. They lean on each other, he says, like blind men begging alms (*bisogna*), whose very appearance craves (*agogna*) pity. In the *Inferno* Dante uses the *agogna* rhyme to describe dream desire, the illusion-making we practice in sleep. Here he uses it to fix a particular kind of waking wretchedness. These are the only two occurrences of the word *agogna* in the entire poem. By repeating *agogna* while in Purgatory, Dante instantly makes the rhyme recall Hell to us and review the pilgrim's progress. It's as if he were rhyming different zones of human experience.

The poem's quickest bittersweet instant is the appearance in Purgatory of the murdered La Pia. She comes like an apparition and says to Dante: "Deh, quando tu sarai tornato al mondo . . . ricorditi di me" ("Ah . . . When you're back in the world, remember me"). The prick of memory—"la puntura de la rimembranza," memory's *bite*—is expressed in that breathy untranslatable particle *deh*. She begs Dante to remember her when he returns to the life that *she* remembers. It's a charge to do what he's in the actual process of doing. Her *deh* contains a world of anxiety and neediness to be heard, borne witness to, reported. The lines have a terrible pity because they're so exact and, in their blunt brevity, summative of an entire life. "Siena gave me life, / Maremma gave me death, and the one who knows this best / with his ring betrothed and married me."

Dante himself utters the same cry when late in the *Purgatorio*, entering the Earthly Paradise, he asks Matelda to come closer to the river that separates them so that he can understand what he hears only as songlike sounds. For all that Dante says throughout the poem about his literary mentors, his ambitions, his own desire to make certain kinds of music—from "rough, screechy words" ("rime aspre e chiocce") to "dolce stil nuovo" elegance— this scene dramatizes the call to a life of poetry, a toil which begins in impassioned but inarticulate music, pure in its way, and then works toward clear meaning. (This may be the source of T. S. Eliot's notion of poetry as a "raid upon the inarticulate.") Sheer sounds, especially for a poet trying to create a primal orchestration of the vernacular, are siren songs, powerfully alluring and sensuous, that have to be shaped into statements. To answer the call, Matelda instructs him, he must first step into two streams: Lethe, which washes away the memory of sin, and Eunoe, which restores to memory good deeds. The one is efficacious only with the other. The episode articulates the mechanics of memory that govern our knowledge of good and evil.

A poet's memory is a whispering gallery of other poets' voices. Who would not want as an early guide a great predecessor who doesn't get in the way, who launches a younger poet into the freedom of his own idiom? Dante's real traveling companion is the *Aeneid*. Apart from the grand schematic of the descent into the underworld, the *Comedy* contains many imitations of that poem. When Virgil bathes Dante's face early in the *Purgatorio*, it's really the blessing and clarifying of a modern poem's aspirations. On the occasions where Virgil reads his mind ("You could cover your face / with a hundred masks and still not hide / even your slightest thoughts from me"), Dante dramatizes the cool but profound and peculiar intimacy that can exist between a master poet and an ambitious successor. Younger poets say, or complain, that they have the music of some long-dead poet in their heads; or that certain lines haunt them only because of the idiosyncrasy of the music, the strange noise familiar words make. Although it's Virgil who calls the pilgrim Dante to his journey, it's Dante the poet of the vernacular who calls Virgil to sponsor and participate in his poem. Leading Dante, Virgil is in a sense remembering himself, living himself back into a version of his own big poem. When, as they approach the Earthly Paradise (with every step, Dante says, he feels more fledged for the flight) Virgil turns the poet over to Matelda and Beatrice, he is setting the fledgling loose into his own visionary independence. His happy announcement—"Your will is now free, upright, and whole . . . I crown and miter you to rule yourself"—is the decree aspiring poets sooner or later need to hear, or imagine they hear, or never hear at all.

SPIT ON ME

In Dante, Dame Fortune turns her wheel and its turnings decide who comes into prosperity and who loses it. She's regally aloof. We try to bring her close, ground her, borrow some of her power to make us less jeopardized by chance. Luck, be a lady tonight. A charm is a way of cajoling reality, lobbying chance and accident our way, getting Dame Fortune to smile on us. Objects sacred and profane can be fortune bearers, talismans to keep us (or our culture) whole and sane. Words, too, curses especially, are verbal amulets, little power packs that ask the gods to take our side or back us up. For the superstitious Roman Catholic culture I was raised in, the repetitions of prayer, of rosary beads and aspirations, were a medium for creating good fortune. The words themselves mattered not so much as the constancy of the repetition, the organic involuntariness of appeal, wonder, and gratitude. But nothing works like the eruptive brevity of a curse to shake another's spirit into fear or remorse. When I left Philadelphia at the age of twenty-one, by leaving behind a widowed mother and younger sister I was violating the culture's code of filial faith and responsibility. My mother's parting words promised—*hoped*—that I'd fail at whatever I attempted and come crawling back home. When Thornton, the Robert Ryan character in San Peckinpah's *The Wild Bunch*, is sprung from a long prison term by a railroad boss on the condition that he chase down his oldest friend who has robbed the railroad's bank, Thornton stares him down and says: "You son of a bitch." He hisses and spits the words. I heard son-of-a-bitching all over the place in my house and neighborhood, but I'd never heard it spoken with such damning, repugnant vehemence. My mother didn't need such vehemence, only the terseness of the wish.

✡

As children we smirked at the mouthy Italian obscenities adults used. We sensed they had some connection to fate and longed for the just occasion to exclaim "Ma vaffanculo," though we pronounced it in the southern manner so that it sounded like *va fangoo.* But just as common was "Ma vaffanabb'" ("Va a fare a Napoli"), which I understood to mean, roughly, "Fuck you and fuck Naples, too!" Ah, nostalgia for the old country. The good life, warm bread, good wine, roasted peppers, and fresh tomatoes. Ah. In the Taviani brothers' movie *Padre Padrone,* as a bunch of young illiterate Sardinian shepherds are being transported to be inducted into military service, we see their haunted landscape, the rugged plains and hills and oak trees. The sound track sings of the lovely old oaks of Sardinia, while the young men, watching the trees recede into the distance, stand in the back of the truck, unzip, and piss in the direction of those noble oaks, the plains, and all the culture of impoverished misery they are happily leaving behind. Whenever I shyly asked my mother the meaning of *Vaffanabb',* she told me it meant "Go to work."

✡

Most families had a horseshoe hanging somewhere in the house. The usual place was on the lintel overhanging the cellar stairs, so that halfway down you passed under the horseshoe's benediction. It was hung with tines pointing down, as I have one hanging from the lintel in the room where I write, which has horrified some visitors—Protestants, usually—because in that position, they say, its good luck drains out. I have a notion that we hung a horseshoe as we did to turn down the devil's horns, to ward off bad fortune. Some families painted them gold. If one was knocked loose or fell, it was a bad omen: the amulet lost some of its protective power. No one of my parents' generation had ever been on a horse or plowed a field with draft horses or sold wares from a horse-drawn wagon. They were the children of immigrant shopkeepers and manual laborers. I think horses were magical, dangerous creatures to them—as they are still to me—though the vegetable monger, the tinker, and for a while even the milkman still peddled their goods from horse-drawn wagons. (The hollow knock of hoofs was a familiar and reassuring predawn sound of my childhood.) The first time I was allowed to hold a horseshoe—before it was installed in the cellarway—the thing felt shockingly heavy and cold. It was like the first time I picked up a handgun. Its authority was weighted but volatile, unpredictable, uncontrollable. The power of belief in its meaning was mysteriously but palpably there, actualized, but also obviously without the authority of the Church and unaccounted for by the Baltimore Catechism I was memorizing at school. I believed in the horseshoe's powers as my parents did: it was tribal necessity, and a clear material manifestation of a communal terror—of bad fortune, in an economy which could ill afford it. Jung says that in many peasant cultures the horseshoe is an equivalent for the horse's foot, that its meaning is apotropaic. ("The analogous effect of the phallus is well known; hence the phalli on gates.") If the horseshoe, or the horse's hoof (and the phallus), share the same magical purpose, it must have to do with fertility, regeneration, continuity. The meanings surrounding its origins in vegetative myths and agricultural societies were simply taken over in an industrial structure. I suppose the place, the tunneled descent into the cellar, was a kind of fertility setting, but what mattered most was the assurance of continuity and regeneration. (By leaving my culture behind, I was disrespecting and violating continuity.) The power of the object was proportionate to the helplessness my people felt in the presence of fate. For me, I couldn't articulate but felt strongly the conflict—a grinding or chafing—between the God of love and redemption through grace I learned about at school and the rough paganism of living in a universe of random force held precariously in check by mortals' efforts to appease the gods, requiring talismans as aids to living in a world of contingency. Without knowing it, I was stretching a membrane of religious orthodoxy over a cavern of pagan mystery. I wasn't then aware of the difference, the doubleness, but I know I've continued to live it out.

✡

Church decorations were power implements. They seemed to me grandiose, partly because my house was austere and drab, but also because statuary, a chalice or monstrance, stained glass and wall reliefs, thrilled me physically. The narratives and sacred anecdotes represented in glass, or in the Stations of the Cross that marked a Way up and down the church aisles, melted to a plain, satisfying sensuousness of forms. The marble reliefs of the Stations were sexy. The pumiced curves of bicep and buttock, the turned foot or muscled thigh or rippling brow were stunning emergencies of flesh. I often imagined reaching out to stroke the tense forearm of a centurion or of one of the women crowding around Christ as he climbs Golgotha. They reminded me of the pale muscular flesh of my parents and relatives, which I was allowed to see uncovered only during brief summer vacations at the Jersey shore. The stained glass images were different, not at all familial or fleshly. They gleamed only by virtue of light originating outside, drenched with a holiness that seemed almost alien to the church itself. More than those voluptuous wall carvings, the figures of disciples and saints in the stained glass, the images of lamb, bull, eagle, and dove, not only begged for a response but dictated the kind of response. They predetermined desire and drained it of its charge, its fever. The remoteness of the Stations, their material self-containment, made desire looser and wilder, more fanciful even. My feelings could play in the space between the stone and my self. During the Good Friday ceremony, a large crucifix was set down by the altar rail (I remember the Christ being about the size of the ten-year-old I was), and like other devotees I approached the image on my knees and kissed its feet. In that moment all my feelings—for the anxiety, the suffering and death, the promise of resurrection and restoration of a life elsewhere—froze in me; I was unwilling to surrender them to an image of Christ that was so grabbily realistic and literal. The small distance of desire between me and the images of the Stations was crucial to my belief. I needed room to work.

My mother suffered from arthritis in her shoulder. She worked on an assembly line and was accustomed to dozens of minor ailments, but this new pain made the simplest and most unaware activity a spike in the joint. Medical treatment gave her little relief. The doctor gave her injections and told her about "the cost of growing old." (Nature, in other words, was *punishing* her for living long and working hard.) Not long afterward she was talking to a man she worked with, whom she respectfully referred to as "the nice nigger." He suggested helping her arthritis with a laying on of hands.

Desperate to be rid of the pain and angry with the dismissive solace of doctors, my mother, a devout and aggrieved Roman Catholic, consented and promised to contribute to the man's small Baptist congregation if the treatment worked. He laid hands on her shoulder, and said: "Lord, drive Satan out of Rita. Drive Lucifer out. Drive him out." The pain ceased and didn't return. Though enormously grateful and astonished, she couldn't tell people about it. Had her healing been in answer to a novena or candles or a Mass said in her name, or effected by one of the spiritualists she often visited, she would have spread the news fast and loudly. But her healing had a strange, fearful source. Its mystery couldn't be normalized by any of the familiar forms of mediation she lived her religious life by. Touched, finally, once, by what she had to call divine power, she was embarrassed.

✪

In the early morning I'd wake before anyone else so that I'd have an hour or so to read books before walking to my grade school several blocks away. Reading was blissfully auroral; school was dutiful, mechanical. I sat in our one parlor chair, a worn mohair that shone under the light of my lamp. Outside, cars revved up, men got a 5:30 start to work, the milkman rumbled past. In the strange swoon of reading, a book cocked in my lap—Freddy the Pig stories, King Arthur adventures, *A Tale of Two Cities*—I watched the textures and bulk of objects change, their intensities dimming or brightening as if reality's temperature was going up and down. The stirring of the words induced it. The wallpaper, the sofa, the Wildwood boardwalk souvenirs like the scallop glass ashtray holding bright nuggets of saltwater taffy, the narrow knickknack shelves displaying ceramic figurines of Alpine shepherds and milkmaids, the devotional statuettes of St. Jude and the Infant of Prague—they quivered like phantasmagoria, fraught but dreamily immaterial. The fever of seeing was the infection of the words I was reading. If I could see the objects now, that boyish, dressed-to-kill Pantocrator or the black-and-white snapshots of aunts and uncles looking out at me from their backgrounds (concrete backyards strung with clotheslines, unforgiving brick house fronts, the wooly air of boardwalks), I know they would look shabby, pathetic maybe, or genteel. But only until imagination's fever brings them back, the spirit of memory reseeing them *toward words*, burning again. The happy Dutch boy plaster figurine happily shouldered his milk-pail yoke. My father went to work while I sat there reading, to paint hospital walls and furniture with Dutch Boy paints. By the door, the milkman left a fresh bottle.

✡

I'm rereading Maupassant after many years, trying to find something, the perfume of another time, a slightly rank perfume, maybe, like fading jasmine. Bookworming and writing, I get interred, and my kitchen, where I work and spend most of my hours, stays unswept, unwashed dishes sigh from the sink, useless unfinished pages look up at me with pity. I catch an odor, essence of dust, mildew, gorgonzola, grease, boiled cabbage, and Lysol, though no Lysol has touched anything for some time. The smell starts to ooze from every porous surface, while I'm in Maupassant, and I think of Ciccio. Cicc', we called him. *Cheech!* When Annie Hall joins Woody Allen in a movie line, he complains about being hassled "by guys named Cicc'," and in the fungal desolations of *Godfather II* Mike Pentangeli's gun thug is called "Cicc'." *My* Cicc' was caretaker of the American Legion post where my father (who sometimes brought me along when I was, I think, ten or eleven) and his cronies drank and where Cicc' doubled as barkeep. I spent a lot of time doing more or less nothing. Cicc' lived in a small low-wattage space where he slept, prepared meals, and stored numerous dusty oddments, war memorabilia mostly: Kaiser helmets, ceremonial swords, cruddy medals, a bolt-action carbine, cartridges (blank, I found out, when one idle evening I loaded one in the breech and, who knows why, pulled the trigger). Cicc's cell held the smell my kitchen's giving off. Held shelves of books, too. (Houses in my neighborhood had few books.) I stroked them as people do fine carpet and pulled something at random, mostly for its feel—plummy velvet cover, satinish endpapers, gold-leaf edging—and started reading, though it was more a simulacrum of reading, skating my eyes across the lines of the page, much as I've been doing today, drifting half-consciously through Maupassant's "Boule du Suif" and "The Horla." So I noodled and dumbly perused until my father, with a lit-up glassy look, said we had to go. I have no memory of what I read, and what I'm reading now isn't throwing flares: the mystery is that some rhythm of the event, the texture of the experience, wove themselves into the Lysol air—the urinals that Cicc' kept immaculate were next door to his room—and into the Tommy Roselli songs pealing from the chrome-trimmed jukebox beside the horseshoe bar. I caught a glimpse of that sanctum a couple of times and still get a little dreamy sitting in any establishment looking at the glacial vodkas, woodland whiskies, psychedelic schnapps, and other macaw colors that double themselves in back-bar mirrors. How superbly literary it would be if the Maupassant of then crushed me of a sudden and became mysteriously the Maupassant of now. Not a chance. Not much is happening. Sorry firefly flashes suggest some dim restoration to consciousness of that originating experience, but it wasn't Maupassant that mattered. It was the activity of reading. I made a lucky find and didn't know it until now.

✡

Blessings. We hardly ever saw grasshoppers in the city. Summer suffocated and stank but also enchanted, for there would be lightning bugs and, once in a while, a grasshopper. The grasshopper's juice was holy oil. When we caught one, we held its head to our palm and chanted: *Spitabacker spitabacker spit upon me.* (The Italian American in that must have been *I spitta in your face, you spitta back in mine.*) If he conferred the blessing, you let him go at once so as not to queer your luck. The other blessing medium was manure. Fruit mongers and milkmen still used horse-drawn wagons. In summer there seemed always to be glistening fresh heaps warming in the street, or dried dung confetti blown by hot gusts. Sooner or later every one of us kids stepped accidentally in one or the other. But a person struck with great unearned luck, we said, must have been rolling in horseshit.

✡

I had nosebleeds, sometimes three or four a week. An elbow tap in a street game could bring one on, but the trouble was that the bleeding wouldn't stop. The dominant taste of my childhood was the beety aluminum tang of blood tickling down my throat. It usually happened without provocation, like a visit. Once, past midnight, the taste really was a taste, my pillow was wet with blood running down my lips and chin. My parents packed my nose with cotton, I sat with my head tilted back, voices scraped above me, I started to choke on the blood dripping through the saturated cotton, so they took me to the hospital. Spilling blood, I believed, was a holy action. From catechism and the liturgy (or from my obsessive, needy distortion of them), I believed blood was the means to redemption. The body was the medium for deliverance. (Hopkins's testimony in "The Wreck of the Deutschland": "Thou hast bound bones and veins in me, fastened me flesh.") Suffering in the nerves, however, was degrading and shameful; the fool weeps for himself in a corner. But for blood to be loosened in me like that was also a chaos that terrified me. Blood was mined with a motion, a drift. In my young consciousness, blood redemption and disorder somehow became weirdly tied together. The New Testament seemed to depict the lives of the disciples as patterned sequences, purposeful and lucid, but I fretted over what must have been the real violence and uncertainty of their circumstances. Later in my life Caravaggio became an exemplary artist because he painted holiness as an uncontrolled fire that burns inside disheveled animals of appetite and blood. Sometimes reality appears in my dreams as a dense white three-dimensional composition, or object in space, composed of pieces that come unstuck, loosened into puzzle-piece fragments that fall away and float into incoherence. It terrifies me, because I know somehow in the dream that the reality I'm viewing is its own site, is my own consciousness, the planetarium of the skull. When it comes undone, it's the whole world, or all I know of the world, bleeding away.

✡

Luck, once, was a lady in grade school. Every few weeks Sister Anna Maria Alberghetti would pass out Picture Study books, thin but weighty pamphlets covered in heavy brown paper. Inside were small color reproductions of masterpieces the diocese approved for ten-year-old minds. It was a great moment, not for the rarity of the experience (true enough in a culture where the only images on walls in most houses were devotional ones and where there were virtually no books) but for the way so much hard, clear fact could be presented, pictured, in a way that seemed to transcend all fact. I wasn't only being revealed to, I was being released into an ether so heliumized I felt goofed. It also primed me, though I had no notion of it at the time, for what would come later, for Bonnard, Van Gogh, Gauguin, and Redon, the ones who skated the skin between inner and outer, matter and spirit. It became my world elsewhere, a life of forms that could bear the force of human feeling. It intimated a world I might be part of. The colors in the images were so much beyond what I knew that they seemed sacramental. Even now, when I look at a painting by Millet I can't separate from my judgment the deep feelings rooted in Picture Study time, when *The Gleaners, The Sower,* and *The Angelus* were dominant images. It's not nostalgia—those pictures were turbulent experiences, ripping me from my familiar world. Though they weren't far from devotional images, they showed great passion for the world of sensation and brute force. I'm moved in similar ways, and my judgment riddled, when I look at Courbet or Van Gogh, because of their coincidence, secular and religious, with Millet. With Van Gogh I always see some sort of devotional passion—manic, sacrificial, elemental, pious. A devotional passion that blows apart liturgical decorum. When I look at Matisse's *Red Studio,* or his big dance murals at the Barnes Foundation, or the Cézanne *Bathers* in the Philadelphia Museum of Art, or Pollock's *Autumn Rhythm: Number 30,* it's still the Picture Study child in me that first cries out to them.

3

CITY DOG

I

The interior of The Clip Joint, a barbershop pocketed on California Street near Polk, is *echt* film noir. Deep shadows hacked by wooden blinds cool the interior and load it with menace. The ten-by-twelve space accommodates one barber chair (a chunky brown command module), two ancient wire-back chairs for waiting customers, and the mirror ledge with its clippers, scissors, brushes, ointments, and cool blue Barbicide cylinder where big- and small-toothed combs stand ready. Whenever I walk past—a duck decoy and two stuffed quail watch from the narrow window—the barber is usually sitting in his big chair, waiting for something to happen, or snipping at an older gentleman's tonsure. It's a marginal enterprise, as I suppose most old-style barbershops now are, and is often closed. How does such a business survive in an inflamed San Francisco economy where commercial property isn't rent-controlled? The Clip Joint's neighborhood at the foot of Russian Hill has gotten a little tonier the past decade. The seediness of Polk Gulch a few blocks south, whose chop suey joints, massage parlors, head shops, and rough-trade dives used to encroach on this neighborhood, has receded a little to give the area a peachier look. Though it's a going, slow-going, concern, The Clip Joint already has the hushed air of a provincial museum.

If you live in a city and watch it—on the ground, not from a car—you notice such things because they're vital signs, and if you love cities, you don't have to love the changes you see but you do have to swing and sway with change, even if you don't approve of what's happening. Not cosmetic but deep cultural change, such as ethnic communities competing for neighborhood business, pushing and displacing each other like molecules. Nothing new here. In his 1890 book, *How the Other Half Lives*, Jacob Riis wrote: "The once unwelcome Irishman had been followed in turn by the Italian, the Russian Jew, and the Chinaman and has himself taken a hand at opposition, quite as bitter and quite as ineffectual, against these later hordes. Wherever these have gone, they have crowded him out, possessing the block, the street, the ward with their denser swarms." Without this shoving-about, this state of motion, a city becomes a diorama, like Disney's planned community in Florida called Celebration, which was actually designed as a diorama inhabited by walking and talking humans, not an alive (and therefore messy and ill-coordinated) town space, but a trophy acknowledging an unchanging and unchangeable American perfectibility. Celebration was designed to create a close-knit community, as if communities could be so designed before they even exist. The houses, promo material says, "are a blend of traditional southeastern exteriors with welcoming front porches and interiors that enhance today's life styles." When its designers created "Market Street," they certainly didn't have San Francisco's Market Street in mind, or the one I knew growing up in Philadelphia. Celebration's Market Street, the promo literature promises, is "a unique collection of charming shops and tempting eateries nestled around a dazzling lakeside promenade; always on the menu at Market Street are flavorful styles, distinctive ambience, and patio dining." This is mostly publicist fat and fluff, but it communicates one version of a public space insulated against change.

Suburbs counterpose minimal movement to a city's pressurized squirminess. If you live in the suburbs, as I did in the early 1990s, you learn to love, or try in good faith to love, commercial and cultural steadiness. But for a city dog, that steadiness produces a nasty reaction—migratoriness. While I lived in Redwood City, a town on the Peninsula south of San Francisco, I took the train to San Francisco nearly every week, just to walk the streets and take things in. My consciousness lived too much in other times and places, in South Philadelphia, natch, and in Bologna, where I'd spent nearly four years. Such migratory desire isn't good for the spirit. It makes for bad medicine, a divided soul, a condition of near derangement that William James wrote about. My notebooks during those years read now like the chronicle of an illness.

Yesterday I was walking down Via San Vitale in Bologna, having just come from Via San Leonardo, the working-class quarter where colors of the stucco house fronts wane through hues of red and yellow and orange. Along the portico people walked briskly, shopped at the unmarked produce stand that just last week was a garage, or swept pavements. Then I ended up on Via San Vitale, which spokes toward the historic center where two medieval towers stand: Asinelli, tall and complete despite the earthquakes that rattled it in earlier times; and Garisenda, Dante's tower, which in his poem gives scale and vertiginous pitch to the figure of the giant Antaeus, leaning over the Pilgrim on hell's floor. Before coming to the towers, I passed my favorite palazzo, Il Fantuzzi, called Il Palazzo degli Elefanti because of the large ornamental carvings of elephants on the façade, a funny and extravagantly oriental decoration on these medieval streets. The years have so eroded the stonework that the elephants' high relief has been planed nearly flat—they look like yesterday's sand castles. The sunlight slanting down through the portico pillars rules the shadows into even parts. The sun dials across the pavements. Smoke, fumes, odors of buses, cigarettes, coffee machines, perfumes and colognes, cheese and salami. A lady pedals by on an ancient bicycle that seems made of wrought iron, wearing a mink coat and kid gloves. I say to myself: This feels like my place. But this isn't my place. I've always been here, and never really so—I feel a little like a stranger wherever I am. Walking down Via San Vitale I'm where I actually am, in Redwood City, California, where there are no redwoods, where there are few tall trees of any kind. Redwood City is famous for having the most moderate weather west of the Rockies; the town's official motto used to be "Climate Best, by Government Test." The elephants look down on me as I say it, shedding their outlines.

✡

No wonder I'm so fond of San Francisco and Bologna, curved topographies (for all their differences) sloping or arcing or radiating from their epicenters. Growing up in Philadelphia, my geographical imagination had no curves. When I looked at the lush gibbous forms of Africa and South America, the fleshy pendant of Florida, the floating debris of South Sea Islands, in my mind's eye they somehow turned into the Philadelphia street plan: grids, equidistant streets, rule-edged north by south and east by west, the rubbery staves of power lines over trackless trolleys, the gleaming iron trolleycar rails. On Sunday visits to my aunts' houses in North Philadelphia, we drove the seven miles straight up Broad Street, with only the semicircular curlicue around City Hall to interrupt that Puritan pursuit. When I finally left the city, I wanted only curves and spirals and bellies and hills—a flexing line extending infinitely in space.

✡

I'll never get used to it, living in a suburb on the brittle crust of the West Coast, migrating once or twice a year to my South Philadelphia neighborhood and its tumultuous seasons. Here, sunshine, earthquake weather, cheaply constructed and ludicrously expensive houses, dense racial and ethnic mix, Spanish spoken everywhere. There, redbrick houses fastidiously kept and tackily decorated by Italian Americans who speak no Italian or only bits of dialect. I feel like my soul has fallen into a cyberspace that blends all those different structures, weathers, languages: the deep brown beaches of Atlantic City with the momentous closed faces of the casinos standing watch; the crumbling cliffs of the western shore with its sea lions and passing gray whales. One March, in Philadelphia, a great thunderstorm comes up. Purple sky, gleaming buds on dark trees. Lightning filaments split the sky in the chutes between skyscrapers, then the rain falls hard and heavy. But it's also something that, pouring down on me, shuts me out.

Some years ago I revisited, for the first time in over thirty years, the neighborhood where I was raised. Watkins Street, a short east-west blacktop moment deep in South Philadelphia, lies some twenty blocks south of the Beaux Arts pile that is City Hall. On its cupola stands the statue of William Penn designed by Alexander Milne Calder (the modernist's grandfather), one hand extended in a peaceful gesture, the other holding Penn's treaty with the Indians. Until 1987, under a gentleman's agreement, no downtown building was raised higher than the crown of his hat. The many high-rises built since then make the Hall look like a desk ornament. Penn's stature didn't matter as much as the foundation legend it represented, the Quaker egalitarianism and equanimity which, when I was young, had long been violated in the observance. My patch, a squared-off block (Penn designed the city on grids to prevent the spread of fire) occupied mostly by first- or second-generation Italian Americans, was solidly racist, though it was a tolerant racism: so long as "they"—across Twenty-first Street slept a quiet working-class black neighborhood—didn't enter or impinge on our culture, everything was fine. The adults around me all remembered that in the early century the "they" in those southern parishes were Italians, and now they weren't "them" anymore. My people were capable of great charity and protectiveness; the men went off to hard jobs while the women watched the kids and policed the precincts. But we were a culture of unreason. The hatred of blacks was one lump in the maggoty mass of irrationality that ruled our lives and that baffled and terrified me.

There on the corner of Twenty-first, the Mason-Dixon line we called it, was Nate's barbershop, where in summer we boys got butch-waxed buzz cuts to deal with the street's huggy heat. There was the Barbicide jar, a liturgical object sharing its altar with a military brush set, a black dispenser of hot shave cream (which in my image-hoard has become Cézanne's black clock), an electric scalp massager, razor, strop, hand towel, bottles of Vitalis, Pinaud's lilac rub, and witch hazel. The Clip Joint has most of those, but the proprietor doesn't have Nate's characteristic elegant extra-long pinky fingernail, a barber's trademark, it was said, which hovered around our heads like a dragonfly as his scissors snicked, an unsettling feminine element in that masculine chamber. (What if one day, violating every norm that defined our sexual identities, Nate painted that nail magenta? Forget that. Forget business.) Every so often black kids would stand outside the big plate-glass window and knock on it with half-ball bats. Except for the one Polish boy from my street, everybody in Nate's had dark hair. Walking down California Street, I pass a Latino, an Asian couple, a pasty-raw homeless gentleman pushing a shopping cart tarped like caravan cargo, a group of black hip-hop kids, a Middle Eastern male, and, reflected in The Clip Joint's window, this here vaguely Mediterranean-looking middle-aged white guy.

In 1958 a single black mother and her child moved from the other side of Twenty-first to our block, next door to us, where the Polack boy lived. It made no difference to anyone that she was self-sufficient, hard-working, congenial. Their blackness poisoned the village well. That's all anybody needed to know. So as a reflex—a reason grounded in unreason—my parents put our house on the market and sold it to a black family. (Our other next-door neighbors, my parents' lifelong best friends, stopped talking to us forever.) We moved to what all considered the "good neighborhood" of North Philadelphia, nearly the same distance north of City Hall as we had lived south of it, in a Roman Catholic parish where the pastor brokered resales of houses to whites only. Some events that marked our three-year North Philly migration: my father is hospitalized for hepatitis and ordered to quit drinking; he and I are in a traffic accident involving a judge's son (the party at fault) who harasses *us* with subpoenas; my parents, when not fighting, lock down in resentful silences; my grandfather, having lived with us since I was born in our condensed Watkins Street house, has to go elsewhere because our house isn't large enough; I come home to find my father alone and unresponsive in darkened rooms or in the basement drinking from a jug only I know is there; my mother wants a better life, so she takes an assembly-line job; we white-flight prototypes now occupy Humiliation House, my mother's assorted resentments a razor-wire perpetual motion device that flays anyone who gets too close; everyone we know thanks our lucky stars we escaped black people; my father dies of liver cancer, my mother in her seething martyrdom gets angrier, I graduate high school, a black family moves in at the end of the block, so we move back to South Philadelphia, farther south than before, into a house smaller than the one on Watkins Street.

So, thirty years later, there I was back on the block. Black folks occupy the entire neighborhood. Many house fronts, once uniform redbrick with granite steps, have been remodeled or brightly pointed, though several also show signs of wear or neglect, and a few have the withered look and purply interior of certain houses I remember from my childhood, the kind that conceal desolation or derangement. But altogether still a well-kept, working-class street. I didn't pretend to be doing anything other than what I was doing, eyeballing my old house and taking in the surroundings. People I passed stared at the only white face thereabouts. I greeted them with respect and they reciprocated. The street's "identity" had changed, its feeling tone hardly at all. What was different was everything else, the larger surround shaped by socioeconomic hydraulics. When I was growing up, at one end of the street stood a grocery store and bakery, at the other a bar, candy store, and Nate's. One corner over from both were a pharmacy, another grocer and candy store, another bar, a sundries shop and laundry. None of those corners, in 2000, was open for business. Shop fronts and windows were covered with sheet-metal cataracts as if to keep a wicked jinn from escaping. A neighborhood corner is a critical place. It fixes compass points that situate the block in relation to the city at large; people gather there and share news, so it stabilizes social relations; if it's commercially vital, it loops back to the neighborhood a sense of well-being. The corner was circulatory energy. It was where our world, minute though it was, stayed in motion, and it made us feel part of that world. It was a gateway to the greater world-in-motion outside—when we village-dwellers went to Center City we said we were going into town—and was also a patrolled frontier where the unwanted or adversarial were denied entrance. South Philly gangs were identified by corner ("Ninth and Carpenter," "Tenth and Christian"), though our block had no gang, only an improvised string of tough boys who occasionally marauded the black neighborhood one block down and beat up kids who reciprocated and jumped us in our own streets.

The energy of change can diminish or vitalize a place, but without it a place atrophies. Corner culture in most cities has dissipated and reconstituted itself in a thinned-out form (but serving the same communal purposes) in mini-malls and short commercial corridors. And while in memory I value the village familiarity and self-sufficiency that corner culture reinforced in those years, I also remember the insularity, repressiveness, fear, and arrogance it encouraged. I've never missed it, but when circumstance has deposited me in other locales, I've missed the feeling of a vital surround that I think of as "city neighborhood." It was no surprise to me in 2000 that the corners were dead spots, not only on Watkins Street but, as I walked farther south, everywhere, except for a couple of convenience stores, accordion-gated, with dim interiors, fronts gashed by graffiti's manic fits of self-mutilation. If this was "signing," a way of claiming and owning a place, it said the neighborhood belonged to the deranged misrule of the streets. If you live on Watkins Street now and need cigarettes or a loaf of bread, you have to take a walk. The only well-stocked market is a dingy supermarket many blocks away.

Close by that supermarket is a street, an island still occupied by Italian Americans, near the President movie house I went to a thousand times as a kid and is now a catering business. I stopped to talk with an old man sitting on his front steps, explained my presence, and, after he overcame his obvious suspicions about conversing casually with a stranger—suspicions I recognized from long ago like a language unused but not forgotten—he drifted into a monologue, hoarse with age, about the deterioration of his neighborhood. But his block looked pristine. The deterioration was everywhere else—he swept his arm like Lear cursing his daughters—and was due to "those people." He couldn't afford to move or he'd have gotten out as soon as *they* began to encroach. I'd passed a barbershop on his corner and asked about it. "He retired a couple of years ago but keeps it like that." I'd looked through the squinty wooden blinds that pinched light into the room. The one magisterial chair—dark green vinyl seat and back racked together by fierce chrome fittings and hand crank—sat on a fat, gleaming hydraulic shaft. On the mirror ledge: Pinaud, witch hazel, and the rest. It was a place out of time that change had left behind, a dandily preserved archeological site nobody visited, and who would want to? A city is made of those who live in it and make it run, but it has its own independent agency, an authority irreducible to material properties. Change and redefinition operate apart from the will of the inhabitants. That's not quite accurate, I know. Economic factors driven by social tilts—gentrification, absentee landlords, government-encouraged small businesses or government-driven attritions—often decide or at least initiate such changes, but redefinition *feels* like a force greater than us. The more vital the city, the more it gives and takes, the more its people come and go. I come and go, every so often, in three- or four-month bursts, for work or writer-in-resident gigs. In 2002 I left San Francisco to live in Berlin for a few months. When I came home and one day was in Russian Hill to buy raw oysters for dinner, I walked down California Street. The Clip Joint was gone, replaced by another small business: "Gustavo Hair Design." I don't expect to be patronizing Gustavo soon, but some clients already are. The old command module has been replaced by three anorexic Eames-ish chairs. No witch hazel in sight, which may be too bad, but as city life goes, all's the better.

3

During the months I spent in Berlin, the regional express I took to central Berlin from Wannsee, the suburb where I was living, passed through Lehrter Bahnhof, a stop that has become a traversal for regional and inner-city rail traffic as well as Europe's largest interchange for its high-speed ICE trains. Only the concrete shelving that would become aboveground platforms had been finished. Also planned was a deep tunnel for the ICE trains and two book-ended multi-use structures enclosing offices and a shopping mall. The bookends are glass boxes, and curved glass panels vault the basilica-size shed. Visible through them are people walking the circular ramps of the glass-and-steel Reichstag dome built in 1996 that replaced the original war-damaged dome demolished in 1954.

The Bahnhof panels, the dome, and the swooping glass canopy covering the Sony Center courtyard in Potsdamer Platz, visible in the middle distance, are all architectural expressions of the transparency that is postwar Germany's political ethic. Preserving an open society has been essential to reconstruction, especially after the wall came down in 1989. I was reminded of this when I walked Wannsee's suburban lanes, lined with villas fancied by the Nazi high command. Up the street from my apartment was a house, hidden from the road, that Goebbels frequented, and not far away is the lakeside villa of the 1942 Wannsee Conference, where Eichmann ("a gelid fanatic," in Primo Levi's perfect phrase) and other murderous mediocrities planned out and gave name to the Final Solution.

When Christo got permission in 1995 to wrap the Reichstag in silver foil, he turned it into a complex metaphor. The icy, opaque draping recalled the impermeability and secretiveness of the Reich, but it also turned a symbol of parliamentary freedoms into a reflecting public showpiece. It flashed back to Berlin an image of itself, toned by a kind of mournful exuberance. The glass dome went up shortly afterward. A Jewish friend of mine is contemptuous of it and other glass signatures around town because all he sees (he says) are reminders of Kristallnacht. There are countering statements. The least transparent structure in Mitte is the Jewish Museum designed by Daniel Libeskind. It's the most aggressive architectural form in town, its ambiguous zigzag shape resembling an unfolded Star of David *and* a storm-trooper lightning bolt. Its zinc exterior has fewer windows than any comparable structure in town, and they're such narrow slashes that you can't see much from them.

After my first glimpse of the Reichstag dome I began seeing glass everywhere. Because I live in earthquake country, I'm skittish about what's hanging over my head. I get nervous just looking at the newest structure on Friedrichstrasse. The façade of the five-story building—traditional height limits have given the city a skyline with a very low center of gravity—is shingled with five-by-eight sheets of glass just waiting, I'm certain, for a provoking autumn wind to peel them loose. Farther up Friedrichstrasse is the big department store, the Galeries Lafayette, glass inside and out, shopping areas deployed around a central conical well so that wherever you are, you can look up and around and see into four floors of merchandise. It's as far as the nineteenth-century French arcade, the prototype for malls, can be taken.

American architecture tells largely a story of capitalist ideology and formal invention. Our urban planning isn't mediated by political history or ethical reflection. The voices debating what to do with the World Trade Center site are addressing issues outside conventional architectural discourse. Should the site become a memorial? What, then, to memorialize, and how to do it in a way that answers to New York's feeling of loss and violation? Whatever gets built should be a measure of the American style of conscience, though it's impossible that America's commercial and commercializing heart will be entirely left out. When a city gives public shape to remembrance, it's choosing how to represent itself to the world and to itself. Much of Berlin's postwar, post-wall reconstruction has been shaped by questions we've seldom had to ask. The wall, all twenty-seven miles of it (plus seventy more separating West Berlin from surrounding East German territories), cut right across Potsdamer Platz, which during the Weimar years was one of Europe's most dynamic, elegant public spaces. In the years after the war, it was a wasteland of dirt, weeds, and rabbits. Just before the wall came down in 1989, the Daimler-Benz Corporation negotiated the purchase of fifteen acres of Potsdamer Platz at one-third to one-seventh of their value. The political left was appalled by the giveaway—Daimler-Benz had worked with the Nazis—and foresaw what came to pass, that a brilliant Mercedes hood ornament would rotate like a perennial Christmas star above what is again becoming Berlin's most famous public space. Daimler-Benz wasn't the only privateer. Sony, too, bought itself a bargain plot. Many West Berliners thought this all a healthy sign of their city's emergence as a powerful post-reunification commercial entity. (Love change, like it or not.) By 1993, land values in Potsdamer Platz had quadrupled, and it was too late to prevent the area from becoming a sort of banal, mixed-use, global corporate cluster doubling as a tourist center, a see-through center.

I've passed through Potsdamer Platz several times, and although the layout is massive and simple, I always feel a little disoriented. It's a cloistered space of a certain kind, an intensification and modernization of the covered arcades of nineteenth-century Paris, which were designed largely to encourage shop-window commerce. Even when I'm outside in the pedestrian zone connecting the buildings, I feel I'm in an arcade. And there is in fact a sprawling *Arkaden* inside one of the buildings, indistinguishable from malls around the world. Glowing faintly amidst the skyscrapers and construction sites is Potsdamer Platz's patient-butler traffic signal, Europe's first, erected in 1925, which in its current setting is a quaint, puny curio.

4

Back from Berlin to the first beatitudes, take them or leave them, of a San Francisco summer, early June, fog breathing west from the ocean on a sunny cold wind, and this city dog is wondering why he doesn't miss the country more. I have a neighborhood friend—he's North Jersey to my South Philly—who actually hates birds. If you're a city soul, you're a provincial. New York smarts, Berlin irony, Roman operatics, Chicago swagger. Big hearts all, with mentalities that tend to extend only as far as the city limits, because who needs more? Sometimes it's not city limits but neighborhoods. Angelenos who love their city—always love-as-strife, love-as-concession, no matter the city—will specify their neighborhood. (L.A. being the protoplasmic organism that it is, by neighborhood they mean landmasses the size of small towns, but never mind.) When I tell a friend raised in smoggy Pasadena about a hotel on Venice Beach I stay in when I visit L.A., he shrugs me off: "That's beach culture, I don't know anything about that." I can usually detect the slight catch in the voice—it's like a poker tell—of someone who says he "comes from Philadelphia" when he's not really *from* Philadelphia, but somewhere nearby, suburban, outlying, a *foreign* place, with grass and driveways, and a golf course probably, Willow Grove, maybe, or Conshohocken.

A city, as an entity larger than its inhabitants, bears an identity pressured into being by those who live and work there but also by externally generated forces, by hearsay and expectation. Visitors say San Francisco is "the most European of American cities," though no one who lives here knows what that means. Is it like Amsterdam? Brussels? It has more to do with a certain familiar style, a speed or mood, or its smallness, I suppose, but even these are bell-jar considerations. The actual place has its own respiratory rhythms, and its breath can be vile. For generations city administrations and business organizations have been helpless to transform a stretch of Market Street that seems mysteriously and irretrievably lost. West of the dolled-up downtown area—Union Square, Macy's, Bloomingdale's, Barneys, multiplexes—the street frays into porn shops, grind houses, army surplus stores, and shop windows stuffed with hundreds of knock-off electronic gadgets. Beyond those, despite the presence of a few tenacious upscale restaurants and antique dealers, Market Street feels edgy and crumbly, listing toward skid row. One night along that stretch I saw a homeless man sitting on the sidewalk, planted in it, he seemed, legs splayed before him, at the entrance of a defunct, boarded-up salsa club that was once a jumping spot but quickly fell to the curse of that zone. The man was liquefying before my eyes, his body a runny fuddle of dark bundled clothes and sooty skin. His pud, hanging from open pants, had spread a glistening delta of piss that was almost iridescent in the early evening light. The media this week is making high hosannas to the memory of the recently deceased Ronald Reagan. Great man, great optimist, great communicator. We cling so hard to whatever falsehood will sustain us in our American exceptionalism, that in the media only the odd spoilsport is reminding us that the former president shredded the social safety net and "de-institutionalized" the mentally ill. Images slip and slide. The smiling Gipper, the man with the peacock piss-streak, semi-comatose, a word I learned when my father was dying, his legs in sour bedsheets spread the very same way, as if he'd never stir again, like that Market Street stumblebum, who reminds me of the destitute mother and child whom the hero in Melville's *Redburn* sees day after day in a Liverpool alley, until one day he finds them replaced by a pile of lime.

I once walked from Venice Beach to Santa Monica to meet friends for dinner, wanting a ground-level view of whatever changes of textures and rhythms that stretch of land (and time) had gone through. I started from my hotel, the Cadillac, an Art Deco-pink elephant with a gondola hanging from the ceiling of its defunct, creepy lounge, after watching a gypsy-ish, four-toed boardwalk performer try to do his act—treading broken glass barefoot while carrying a tourist on his back. His St. Christopher routine broke down when the passenger, a double-wide, got hysterical on the way up and nearly brought them both crashing down. An hour or so later, when I told my dinner companions I'd walked all the way, straight down Main Street to Santa Monica's posh Third Street Promenade, they were alarmed, then relieved to hear I hadn't been mugged. From cozy, shabby Venice Beach I'd passed through a young, fast-moneyed strip of restaurants and shops that sold subtle ugly pottery and other classy geegaws in upscale bad taste, then some less illustrious blocks of apartment buildings and houses, then a stretch near Ocean Park—where I was supposed to have been mugged—lined with locked gates or boarded windows and doors like my old Watkins Street neighborhood, where DMZ convenience stores and a few active businesses like locksmiths and washing machine repair shops cruise the bottom of the commercial feeding chain alongside "Check-Cashing & Bill Pay," "Yancey's Pizzeria," and "Uno Dollar Store."

Keats, Baudelaire, and Rilke were all serious city walkers and watchers, a little dandified in that they were aware of foraging, keen on life as material, life which happens to be the medium of existence, "the 'I,'" as Baudelaire described the dandified flâneur, "seeking to be lost in the 'not I.'" Joseph Cornell haunted Fourth Avenue to collect the material he put inside boxes that enshrined ambiguous visions of journeys not taken, hotels not visited, personages not met. He collected to reimagine. Cities offer up casual happenings and visions that come and go, perfect (and odd) in their moment, that slip into the stream of stuff cities feed on. In a 1947 journal entry, Cornell mentions spotting a young girl on a Madison Avenue bus:

> Plain black dress flowered trimming white thin strip around neck and down center of dress. She had a book under her arm, "Little Women" and traveling alone. Alert, quiet, assured, and modest (brown hair, a

countenance not pronouncedly pretty but of manner always evoking a sadness that will only see her for a moment or so and then never again). (A beautiful innocence.)

What makes this so acutely of-the-city are the parentheses, that what happens *right there* is always off to the side, spoken with the head bowing.

5

This summery day I've been walking Golden Gate Park. Disco roller-bladers were line-dancing and spinning through ovals and figure eights on a patch of macadam near the Conservatory, the park's flower cathedral. The eucalyptus trees were waving medicinals, young parents pushed wheelbarrow double-strollers, the foxgloves and bluebells and pittisporum (sweetest of the sweets) were in bloom. But the city thrill was to leave the park, head toward the N-Judah stop at Ninth and Irving, and step into a streetcar drippy with saloon fumes, some sort of carnival in progress, loud voices and CD players, and I now remember that earlier today was Bay to Breakers, an annual benefit run from the eastern end of town to the ocean, some twelve miles, which started years ago as a serious race for serious runners but has become a little like the clown division in the New Year's Mummer's Parade in South Philadelphia. Among the serious runners are goofball contingents like Gay Cowboys for Peace; multisegmented, noncompetitive creatures like caterpillars and tapeworms; hundreds of nude runners, some body-painted, whom the city allows to display their goods only until they reach the finish line, beyond which they have to dress immediately or risk a two-hundred-dollar citation. And inventive individuals like those on my streetcar: a skinny kid wearing a spiked dog collar and grass skirt; another sporting a Daredevil costume that sagged sadly in just those spots that should have been muscled up; a "hard hat" whose helmet supported a bladder of beer which Mr. Tough Guy—chief source of the alcohol sourness—could siphon into his mouth through coiled cherry-colored tubing; a stout bravo flashing at nearby females his rubber-chicken codpiece; and two plump girls, twins, in raspberry wigs, dead asleep, tipped slightly against each another, inert like children deep in dreamland. A voice, singing softly along with some girl-group song rolling from a portable CD player, is joined by two more voices, then others, until a sluggish choral animal is moving heavily but sweetly, so sweetly, through nearly every sagging body at my end of the car:

> Well it's a Saturday night, you know the feeling is right,
> Don't you know we'll get so high.
> Get down get deeper and down,
> Get down get deeper and down,
> Saturday night.

ROCKING AT THE CADILLAC

The Second Fork

Every morning during a stay in Venice in 2001, I thought of Rigoletto. Forget that he belongs to the court of the Duke of Mantua. His plush red-and-white coxcomb was practically the first thing I saw when I opened the shutters, along with velveteen, parfaited Dr. Seuss Cat-in-the-Hat hats, Mad Hatter plugs, and Uncle Sam stovepipes, all bobbing and swaying on vendors' carts pushed along by a couple of my neighbors on their way to St. Mark's. Jangling like costume jewelry was the more classic junk: gilded plastic gondolas; I ♥ VENICE headbands; pint-size Italian flags; tin miniatures of the great bronze horses brought to Venice from Constantinople in 1204; and other hats. Sales seemed to split along national lines. Non-Italian tourists favored the beribboned, regulation-issue gondolier's boater. Italian schoolkids, shrieking gangs of them on cultural outings, went straight for the florid headgear.

Though just a minute's walk from St. Mark's, my apartment was on a secluded double cul-de-sac reachable only through one of those enclosed passageways they call a *sottoportico*—"under the portico": *pordego* in Venetian dialect. I'm an early riser. The first sounds I heard were the thump of closing doors and the clock of cartwheels on cobblestones. Then canaries singing in cages outside high windows. And people going to work, whistling, singing, humming. So many windows opened onto my street (Corte Contarina Ramo II, "Second Fork of Contarina Court") that any street whistler or singer had a theater right there. Because there are no cars or buses or motorbikes, you can hear yourself and others making tuneful sounds. It's pleasurable to know that the resonance in your head is being not only voiced but heard.

If I'm So Clever, Why Don't I Understand Anything?

The Venetian accent has a certain sweetness that turns *ciao* into a three-syllable, three-toned word, something Chinese. Venetians also commonly speak to each other in dialect. Dialects aren't accents but complete languages more or less distinct from standard usage, changing not only from city to city but from small town to small town. Italy has hundreds of them. Linguists travel around to collect and record them. Bologna, where I lived for a few years, has its own, which in its French inflections must carry over something from Napoleon's occupying armies. My Italian serves me pretty well, but in my barbershop, when Otello, whom I thought of as the Moor of Venice living in exile on Via dell'Inferno, was chatting with clients and cronies— they'd gossip and smoke while he laid his straight razor on your Adam's apple—I understood next to nothing. My Bolognese friends tell me that dialect usage is dying there and in other prosperous northern cities because the young aren't interested in learning it. In a world where cultural differences keep breaking down into an American-generated uniformity, young people are less inclined to adopt the linguistic subculture of their parents. Wherever I walked in Venice, however, I heard teenagers speaking dialect, rolled and gulped in an accent that pulls vowels down the throat as if they have to be held back in order to be expressed.

Kill That Moonlight!

Preserving dialect goes along with Venice's island character. Dialect is still strong in Sicily and Sardinia, but those islands don't belong to the world. Visitors, Anglophones especially, feel a sense of entitlement in Venice, *to* Venice. (Imagine feeling entitled to Naples.) There were always foreign populations passing through or settling in *il lagunare*, as the papers like to call it, because of its commercial and geopolitical position in the Byzantine

Empire and the Renaissance. The quay near the Doges' Palace is named Riva degli Schiavoni after the Slavs (*schiavoni*) from Dalmatia who sailed, traded, and settled there. By the nineteenth century Venice had acquired its modern character as a civilization under glass, where Europeans came to see and be seen. It was already a jewel box civilization, though even then if you opened the lid you smelled something spoiling. By the early twentieth century it had become a conspicuous, prized symbol of the present-as-past. The Futurists, that group of noisemaking artists and writers active from 1909 to 1915, wanted to force Italy into the new age of machines, speed, and mechanized violence. They hated Venice and coined the word *passatismo*, past-ism, to describe the cult of a preserved, idealized past that Venice represented. It was Venice's subtly lit, picture-framed evenings they had in mind when they titled a manifesto *Let's Kill Moonlight*. They failed at that. Now it's the world's monocultural bazaar, an open air mall-cum-museum, moonlit if you please, that serves millions as a vision of history fixed in time. In recent years the municipal government has actually considered charging admission to the city.

From its early days as small, scattered settlements around the lagoon, Venice has been a place of craftspeople, merchants, and traders. Other Italians respect Venetians' commercial canniness and take for granted the secretive nature of their culture. They can seem outgoing and exuberant *because* their society is so secretive. The more they seem to offer their city to others, the more they keep it to themselves. My overwhelming feeling for Venice is that it gives and withholds itself at the same time, concealing its private life in its extraordinary public life. Its architecture illustrates this: the stately theatrical façades along the Grand Canal seem designed to mask another identity. The whistling vendors of my Second Fork are maskers, too; they share privacies of the city that none of us can know. Venice slips attempts to represent it. Like Rome, New York, and Paris, it's among the most written-about cities in history, a place of which nothing remains to be said, therefore everything remains to be said. But what to say and how to say it? One day in the Piazza San Marco I watched a young man with a camera trying to line up a shot. He found a spot, checked the viewfinder, then without snapping the picture moved to a different spot and went through the same routine. I watched him test at least a dozen points of view before he finally gave up. He wanted what we all want: an original, fresh, personalized angle. But San Marco is cut to the same pattern as the Venetian character: its trapezoidal plan, widening as it approaches St. Mark's Basilica, opens up the space while the arcades siding the piazza contain and compress it. And the clear sight lines we should have of the breadth of the marbled basilica and Doges' Palace are blocked by the red brick campanile. The more the piazza seems to open to our view, to be a space with no secrets, the more it folds back into itself. San Marco may be the most photographed public space in the world, but every picture of it replicates an illusion. Take a picture and you record today's mask. If you're really trying to *find* something with a camera's eye, you end up not really viewing the piazza or the loggia or the basilica; you're looking at all the failed attempts to discover something the place withholds. You lose yourself in a million perfectly respectable and completely unoriginal images that fill the air between your eye and its object. That young man, unlike most of us, realized how futile it was even to try.

Rocking Chairs

I've never taken a gondola ride, though one of my favorite spots in Dorsoduro, the southern branch of land that has the hardest clay substratum in the islands (hence *dorso duro*, "strong spine"), is an old gondola repair yard called in dialect a *squero*. Gondolas have to be scraped and tarred every few weeks. This particular *squero* now turns up in guidebooks, so what was once a quiet work site, where overturned hulls create a lacquered black light, has become another itinerary stop. Years ago, even before it became fearsomely expensive to take a gondola tour, I thought I was above such crass tourist lures. Callow and stupid youth! The best way to see the city historically, of course, is to see it the way we look at murals and ceiling decorations, *da sotto in su*, looking up from below, the way Goethe and Casanova and Byron and James and so many others saw it. So I've promised myself next time, if there is a next time, to ride in a gondola, if somebody else treats. Most get around on *vaporetti*, the water buses which on Easter Sunday, the official beginning of high season, remind me of old front-page images of boats tipsy with Albanian refugees chugging toward Brindisi. My favorite way of getting around is by *traghetti*, the very plain gondolas that ferry passengers across the Grand Canal, sparing you the effort of walking to the nearest bridge. You pay your minuscule fare, stand to face the landing, then push off and come around to face the opposite bank. It's a commonplace, and like most commonplaces disturbingly true, that a *traghetto* rock-a-bye-ing across the water with its file of unspeaking passengers looks like a boatload of souls crossing the river Acheron in Dante's *Inferno*, though Venetians don't show the perverse anticipation to arrive as Dante's shades do.

Whenever I'm in Los Angeles I stay in Venice at the Cadillac Hotel, a pink stucco Art Deco slab right on the beach. I feel at home in its weary Eurotrash ambience, and I love the gondola hanging upside down above the bar like a mad emperor's baldachin. In 1904, when Abbott Kinney used his cigarette fortune to buy 160 acres of marshland, his vision was to create an American equivalent of *la serenissima*. He dug nineteen miles of forty-foot-wide canals and bought Italian-made gondolas to put in them. (Without them people might have mistaken Venice for Delft.) The Cadillac's is one of the few left. By the 1920s the canals had become so miasmal and smelly that most had to be closed. In the 1960s there was a small run on original gondolas by Texas oil magnates. Who knows what became of them? There are genuine gondolas once again among us at the Venetian Hotel in Las Vegas. Venice, Italy, is built on millions of wood piles driven into a hundred feet of mud resting on a heavy clay bed that floats on peat and watery sand. (It actually is the illusion it creates: a floating city.) The Venetian is built on the Sands, imploded in 1996, where Jerry Lewis sang "Rock-a-bye My Baby." Gondolas cut their mild wakes along the Strip in a canal of recycled water that goes nowhere and in the "Grand Canal," which runs down the center of a shopping mall. Since most of the guests are there to gamble, *traghetti* would be more appropriate. I'd pay to see that. The Futurists, bad boys that they were, called gondolas "rocking chairs for idiots."

Go Slow

Gondolas, *traghetti*, *vaporetti*, speedboat water taxis. What is a person to do for cabbie talk? A Roman cab driver's oratory—I had just come from recondite, self-contained Venice—pumped me up for dealing with that explosive city. When I told him I was from San Francisco, he wanted to talk food. Never having been to America, he's sure he could never eat our food. When I tell him that our cuisine, most of it, comes from somewhere else, *anywhere* else, he shrugs. When I ask him about the "slow food" movement launched in Italy several years ago to counter the cult of fast-food restaurants, he said it couldn't be true, that there can't be such a thing as a "slow food" movement because Italian culture is incapable of permitting fast food. (There was already a McDonald's at the Spanish Steps, but never mind.) He kept shaking his head and squinting at me through the rearview mirror. "Where did you hear about this so-called slow food movement?" "I read about it in the *New York Times*." Ah! Well, there it is. Newspapers! They'll make you believe whatever they want you to believe. Within minutes we had left slow food and insidious newspapers and he was presenting, declaiming really, a lament that he had obviously devised and refined into a grievously sage aphorism. Rome has changed terribly, for the worse, and to think we were once a great ancient power. This used to be a city where all Romans were actors in this great theater, who expected millions of spectators to come from around the world to watch the performance. Now our *Roma* has become a huge theater with many spectators but no actors.

The closest I've come in Venice to such forensics was when I asked a guard at the Scuola di San Giorgio degli Schiavoni—more about this exquisite place in a moment—where I could get a bite to eat without paying an arm and a leg. Italians say "without paying an eyeball from my head." (The divine Marcello once called an interviewer's attention to his new shoes: "Queste scarpe mi hanno costato un occhio dalla testa!") The guard went on at tortuous length refusing to offer advice. Why? Because Venetians are all thieves! Restaurant owners most of all, and besides, it's hard even to find a decent place to eat. I persisted. He carried on. The more he talked, the less he divulged, until finally, with excruciating caveats, he gave me an address where I might (or might not) get good food but where in any case the people are all thieves. Thus I found a smallish trattoria jammed with a tourist lunch crowd. Because I was alone the waiter squeezed me into a small booth next to a German couple. When he tossed down the menu (they were serving slow food fast), I told him without looking at it that I wanted a plate of spaghetti with seafood—whatever the kitchen was producing—and a salad. Isn't the *signore* having a *completo*? No, I'm not. The *signore* may not have a meal here unless he orders a full course. Excuse me, but this is a *trattoria;* you serve the food, I pay for it, and I'd also like a half carafe of white wine, please. I'm sorry but we can only serve full-course meals. I refused again and got the bum's rush, Venetian version. I thought about doubling back for a chat with the guide at the Scuola but remembered that by now he'd be at home enjoying a full-course meal of slow food.

Carpaccio and Basketball

The *scuole* were lay confraternities based on trade/craft or nationality that performed services for the church such as tending to the sick and the poor. The Scuola di San Giorgio degli Schiavoni is my favorite indoor space in Venice. I've been there several times, yet whenever I step across the threshold I feel the force of it as if for the first time. I feel safe, truly and rightly "housed" there. Its intimacy is intensified by the paintings of Vittorio Carpaccio—his "raw beef" red gave the dish, invented at Harry's Bar, its name—that cover the walls and wrap themselves around your consciousness. The two famous pictures are *St. George Slaying the Dragon* and *St. Augustine in His Studio.* On this recent visit, I was reminded how you can know a painting by heart, or think you do, and be struck by a familiar detail as if you've never noticed it before. On the field where St. George kills the dragon—his lance spikes through and shatters behind the monster's skull—and where the chewed-up remains of sacrificed boys and girls litter the dirt, there's a beautifully artic-ulated skeletal trunk and head sitting upright, paying attention. What hit me hard this time is that it's projecting its deadened gaze beyond the plane of the picture, looking straight at us, at me, like an admonition or invitation.

In the St. Augustine picture, Carpaccio made one of the great portraits of a writer. Its light looks like a liquid element in which the entire image is suspended. Augustine is at his desk composing a letter to St. Jerome at the very moment of Jerome's death, announced by light pouring through the window just above his head. Across the room, in a low corner, sits a fuzzy, alert pooch, a cutie with a postcard all his own. He's part of the pattern of creation that includes Augustine, Jerome, and we who regard the picture. The pooch, too, takes notice of the light. Depicting Augustine looking up from his work out the window, Carpaccio gives us a severely joyous image of a writer's expectation, attentiveness, and availability to bestowals and visi-tations. Paying attention is a form of waiting, and Augustine is an enfleshed expression of the skeleton's attentiveness in the St. George picture.

That night I paid attention to Italian basketball on television. I remem-bered a time when Italian high school boys learning organized basketball were forbidden to talk while playing. I've watched playground games where but for an occasional *grande* shouted after a basket or *fallo* after a foul, you wouldn't know a game was going on except for the scraping of rubber and the rattling of the hoop. This elegant, dire quiet translates into the way tape-delayed NBA games used to be broadcast in the days before satellite and cable: game sounds were muted so the players seemed to skate up and down court on a thin ice of sound. The color man was king because his was the only voice we heard. Italian ball is the same game played in a different style, with a different kind of gaiety. We're used to the banging American whoop-whoop style. It's the playground decorum we learn as kids. Italian players can be as tough and driven as anyone, but their court decorum lies close to a cultural norm: *fare una bella figura*—to look good, to cut a figure. Italian ball, I have to say, can be pretty weak coffee, though it has improved along with the rest of the international game and, like many other countries, has channeled gifted players to the NBA. In the not so very old days, too many field goals were the result of an obvious advantage, like a big center or a guard who could break down a defense, but in recent years Italian clubs have distinguished themselves for the hustling team play and toothy defense that have caused pan-European teams to defeat the one-on-one American style in international competition. (Though the most abrasive, petulant one-on-one NBA player, Kobe Bryant, grew up and developed as a player in Italy.) Some aging NBA players (like Kobe's father) finish their careers in Italy, where even a dodgy veteran is valued. I once saw a news story on Bob McAdoo, an NBA iron man who played out his last few years in Italy. When coaxed by an off-camera voice to speak some Italian for the viewers, he smiled and growled: "Mmmmm, pasta!"

Get Lost

Wherever I travel, whether to Venice, California, or the other one, I don't so much take in images as images take me. I'm aware of storing pictures in memory, of course, but when I recall them they become a wraparound environment, a climate of consciousness. I'm indiscriminate and don't sift high from low, refined from rough. My mental picture of the four-toed broken-glass walker on Venice Beach, trying to heft onto his back a woman built like a Wagnerian soprano, is as all-covering, so to speak, as the one of a dolphin pod passing just offshore. Remembering is like standing in the center of the Pantheon, though the walls and vault are coated with images of the prostitutes I saw at 1 A.M. on the periphery of Verona, or the conic shape a light rain took as it fell in Siena's famous Campo, where the Palio is held, or the big-mouthed, big-tongued sea monster giving up Jonah in a ceiling painting by Tintoretto. Even when I'm already in a place, I'm longing to see it, really see it, to take in all its details in one composite instant of perception while able in the same instant to isolate any fragment. Every place has its own natural history, some pattern of changeful progress that explains everything from the rising waters that periodically inundate San Marco to the superb lacework of Burano to the architectural eccentricities of the Ghetto Nuovo, where tenements were built up and strangely articulated with punched-in loft spaces—the buildings there, as nowhere else in town, look squashed—to accommodate the growing Jewish population. When I have dreams of a perfect city, its completeness and coherence show itself like an exoskeleton. I dream constantly of cities, familiar and otherwise. Sometimes I see Bologna as a completely articulated form in space, like a Calder mobile. As often as I've been to Venice, I've never dreamed about it, though I think of Venice when I look at Joseph Cornell's boxes, because it's a hall of mirrors of suggestiveness. As a mental entity Venice is practically invisible, or its nature is so infused with masquerade that to see it is not to really see it. When I'm standing by the water, especially along the Dorsoduro quay called the Zattere, I feel I'm standing on a horizon line sealing the Venice that rises from the islands to the Venice that's inverted in the mirror of the water. Sometimes the entire city seems like a horizon. Its rooflines and water are where the upper reaches of reality seal themselves to what's here, to where we are. Cities like Rome and Bologna allow your imagination to project beyond what the eye takes in. Venice does not. Looking seaward, it's hard to imagine a sea, a space, any spur of reality beyond what the eye takes in. The great eighteenth-century painter Francesco Guardi made views of Venice in which the water and palazzos, the quayside or piazza activities, become all one membranous horizon.

Venice fools the eye in so many ways. Streets and canals look alike. Every dead end looks like another. One tiny deserted *campo* with a capped well might be any other. Filmmakers love this. Paul Schrader's *The Comfort of Strangers* most disturbingly creates an illusion of the illusion. The nauseating disorientation experienced one long and fateful evening by the two main characters, a young couple struggling with their relationship, who keep losing and then finding their way only to discover that what seemed like the rediscovered right way was just another dreadfully wrong way, is not only true to life, it's true to the *idea* of Venice. Movies love the veil of imminent catastrophe draped around the place. To prepare a friend for her first trip, I took her to see Nick Roeg's jittery *Don't Look Now* and the Schrader film, which I guaranteed would prime her for Venice's water-lit moodiness. "Why are you taking me to movies," she asked, "in which the male lead gets his throat slashed with a straight razor, either by a dwarf in a red raincoat or by Christopher Walken?"

What's for Lunch?

A friend of a friend invites me to lunch at his apartment, which occupies the entire floor of a sixteenth-century palazzo fronting the Grand Canal. Heavily brocaded Asian tapestries, Persian carpets, a bed canopy of Venetian lace and North African silk, ancient gray-visaged mirrors. The apartment reminds me of Christopher Walken's in *The Comfort of Strangers*. One room opens into another, and suddenly we're in the kitchen with its two-inches-thick, rough-cut, marble slab tabletop, or the "Salon," or the atrium containing the harpsichord and grand piano and harp. I spent three hours there and left, like so many visitors to Venice, more disoriented than when I arrived. Then again, for lunch he offered vodka. I like vodka. It fills you like food. Having lived in Venice for nearly thirty years, nothing surprises him. And having been vocal coach and/or companion to Joan Sutherland, Maria Callas, Barbra Streisand, Ethel Merman, and Judy Garland, his stories are endless and his timing perfect. For him the "magic" of Venice that so many people cherish has rusted away completely. I suppose he's as Venetian as any American can become—cynical, weary, socially deft, professionally gifted though perhaps not quite at the top of his game, and an unapolo-getic sensualist. I told him about my visit to the Carpaccio room and my full-course-meal story. "The restaurants used to be fair, never great, but now they're all awful, and I never set foot in Harry's, it's become so vulgar and Eurotrashy. It used to be a place where you could actually have a conversation."

From his balcony he has, or used to have, a view of the old La Fenice (The Phoenix), Venice's great opera house (recently rebuilt and reopened), which on January 29, 1996, he and many others watched go up in flames. Or rockets. The resins concentrated in dry, centuries-old timbers turned them into bombs waiting for a match. The Venetian city government has a lot to protect, if not more than Rome and other great towns, then at least a different kind of patrimony. Rome, Bologna, Naples—these cities work hard to be vital contemporary places while also preserving remnants of their ancient past. Venice is preserving the urban equivalent of a partially restored version of *Gone with the Wind*—it's fixed in time, and its serene stillness belongs to the world. My vodka chum said that when the city government decided to renovate the Fenice, it drained the surrounding canals for dredging (in order eventually to facilitate access—this is the awful irony—by Venice's emergency boats), knowing very well that fires in Venice most often occur during renovations, because of all the antiquated, exposed rewiring. And so when a fire was ignited in the theater by faulty wiring, there was no way for fireboats to reach it. The torch burned for nine hours. When helicopters finally arrived, they had only the equivalent of water balloons to fight the flames. My host and Venetians all over town stood on balconies and watched what looked like a fireworks display.

When I stood to leave at around 4 P.M., the vodka had me swinging and swaying with Sammy Kaye, though my friend seemed to be just getting warmed up. He saw me off with a mighty peroration: "Venetians! Penny pinchers! Thieves and cheats! Don't ever trust them! A great people, but very corrupt, essentially dishonest, but you have to give it to them, they're a people who knows what's what. Poor bastards. Can't blame them. History made them that way." I was so goofed that I left without telling him that earlier in the day, after returning from my morning's shopping at the Rialto market, I discovered that the vegetable monger had shorted me the zucchini I'd asked for—it's wise to eyeball the merchandise from bin to hand to bag—and that the fruit vendor had stiffed me two blood oranges and three bananas.

ON PHOTOGRAPHY

In its childhood it was already a memory garden of antiquities, of ruins and monuments, of pyramids and temples and exotic locales. The technology of the big square-view camera and its delicate chemically treated plates required long exposures, which in turn determined subject matter. But when we look at Maxime Du Camp's "The Colossus of Abu Simbel," where a human figure slouches minutely against the shoulder of the huge pharaonic pile as a measure of its immensity, we can feel photography's rapture for mass. The desire to "view" a piece of civilized antiquity or ancient wilderness was a memory act to interrupt the world's procession before the eye and ritualize its moments. It turned every subject into an artifact. It was a fossil language that recorded the race's earliest memories, the relations between mortals and gods. Carleton Watkins and Eadweard Muybridge's photos of the Yosemite wilderness preserve an archaic vision of the universe's design: the ether separated from the underworld by the earth platform on which the work of civilization occurs. Like Frith and Du Camp, they were just making pictures, and having an adventurous time of it, too. (Early photographers were a mongrel frontier company of adventurers, inventors, chemists, gentlemen of leisure, and at least one murderer.) But the instinct behind that documentarian activity was to steal from time the image of a relation that time itself determines. Timothy H. O'Sullivan's 1873 "Indian Pueblo, Zuni, New Mexico, View from the South" narrates an American genesis. Ladders run like pickets along the terraces of stacked adobe apartments, and thatched lean-tos spike heavenward across our line of vision. A Zuni myth tells how the sky god Awonawilona, mixing his flesh with water, compounded into existence Mother Earth and Father Sky, who then conceived all life in the womb of the earth, out of which emerged the first human beings. O'Sullivan, manipulating the time-absorptive machinery of photography, fixes a memory of human tenancy and stewardship. He had worked with Mathew Brady, and "A Harvest of Death," taken after the Battle of Gettysburg, shows the devastations of that stewardship. Four corpses on a stubble field seem to have been newly shaped out of that same ground and soon to be reabsorbed by it. The picture documents and remembers the death of nature. One doesn't have to believe in divinity to believe that forms generated by the traditional religious imagination have determined the directions and contents of consciousness.

✪

Early photographers were in thrall to the wholly available innocence of their subjects, and their craft was at such an early stage of development that their own curiosity inhaled some of that innocence. The image represented the apparently unmediated encounter between photographer and subject. (Photography soon became also the most brutally sardonic witness to that encounter.) One of the most endearingly spooky images ever made is Fox Talbot's 1840 calotype "Articles of China," included in his pioneering book *The Pencil of Nature.* On the four shelves that occupy the frame sit cups, tureens, saltcellars, bowls, vases, and other bric-a-brac. A startling fresh-ness beams forth from them, they are such pure offerings to the gaze of consciousness. Milk pitcher, squat crystal vases, ceramic figurines of a country lad and maiden holding flowers—they possess a presentness undis-turbed by any history of use. No object has the enfolded, flexed surfaces that might draw us into the life of those stilled forms. Talbot's little things arrive in their image moment with no natural history. This purity of presence is another mystery photographers try to document: the look of things as if they'd never been seen before, never possessed by consciousness.

✪

In 1862 Nadar (born Gaspar Félix Tournachon and an acquaintance of Baudelaire, Delacroix, and Ingres) made a series of images of the Paris sewers and catacombs. (He really drew the compass of the photographic enterprise: he also took the first aerial photographs.) The direction of *his* imagination was not so much toward the electrical light source transported (at great expense and, in 1862, superhuman effort) from the overworld, as toward the look of the space where man-made contrivances—the struts, frames, and braces that organize the underworld for practical use—resolve to oblivion. In one image we see lopsided archways telescoped down toward a nearly perfect rectangle of blackness. Light is sucked away by the void at the center of those braces. Gouging channels in the earth, opening passageways and crafting retainers, is an analogue for intellection—Nadar is giving form to the desire to know.

The starkness with which photography represents disorder is charged and shocking because it works with the given fact of the scene. A painter works to master subject. A photographer's work depends on the willingness to *be* mastered. In Nadar's own time, Watkins and Muybridge (the murderer) were becoming archivists of the pristine jumbled orders of the wilderness. In Watkins's images especially, we see at once how diversity—the finest inflections of mass, height, and girth in a stand of pines—resolves into magnificent likenesses. Within the blocked-out uniformities of pines are countless differentiations of sunlight stripping and exposing the textures of bark, branch, canopy, needle. The tangled disarray of untouched wilderness presents itself as huge jarring harmonies. In Watkins's Yosemite pictures, the sharply defined entanglements of moss, grass, streambed, brush, and gully create a webwork that strikes the eye as a haphazard interfusedness so meticulously designed that the mind, acquainted with contingency and becoming, strains against that vision. Conspicuously *not* knit into that world stuff is the figure. When human beings appear in Watkins's images, they look like not very bountiful sacks of potatoes, all sags and burlap bulges.

✡

Sometimes photography sees the human as material reality grown from or worked into a place, not merely inserted as a measure of the surround. Some of the most astute and unforgiving visions have come from Robert Frank and Paul Strand. When I first saw Frank's *The Americans* in the 1960s, it had already become an alternative American album. Its images had acquired a primitive religious force among college students like myself. We passed around our one battered copy and quarreled over its images, whose disquieting guilelessness seemed not irony but a chewed-up innocence. The locales were nearly as exotic as Lampur and Madura: Arizona, New Orleans, Mississippi, and (for a South Philadelphian like me) Hoboken. And yet for all the moody angularity of the images, we recognized a distinctly American feeling, maybe because as a people we feel—like to feel, anyway—that we're always arriving at new recognitions of our strangeness.

In 1955 and 1956 Frank traveled the country, taking over twenty thousand pictures from which he selected and printed one thousand. Of these, eighty-three found their way into *The Americans*. His street-smart technique involved jarringly cockeyed angles, wooly focus, and perversely obscure lighting. He once told a friend that people who look at his pictures should feel as they do when they want to read a line of a poem twice, and sequencing images was his way of creating the stanzaic continuities of poetry. I once saw an exhibition of *The Americans* that displayed the pictures in Frank's original ordering. A repeated motif could bear dreadfully different feeling tones. In the first image, the Stars and Stripes waves between two grimy Hoboken tenement windows, a figure darkly visible behind each. The flag in a later image shimmers like an enormous shoo-fly above children at a Fourth of July celebration, and again as bunting rising like Victory of Samothrace wings behind a tuba player at a political rally. In Frank's pictures, light—fractured, plumped, mashed—occupies space like a memory of matter: sunshine fizzes on a tabletop in a diner; an irradiated glow swells from jukeboxes. Frank rejected the faked hauntings and woozy auras of art photography and turned nervousness and uncertainty into photographic virtues. His kind of straight photography insinuated itself into the way we view and recall reality. It kidnapped modern consciousness.

✪

Another book we read and quarreled over was *Let Us Now Praise Famous Men*, less for the spongy pathos of James Agee's prose than for Walker Evans's pictures of impoverished Alabama tenant farmers. Evans's vision was more concentrated and "naturalized" than Frank's. He documented faces whose adult ages were often impossible to guess. Everything and everybody seemed used up. Evans is a cool artist; we never feel his view kneaded or roughed into the scene, even when he later snapped pictures from under his overcoat of New York subway riders. His pictures have the almost ingenuous vernacular aloofness of the signage he so loved to photograph. He practiced a rich plain-style poetry, humble yet avaricious. His camera was a stylus that drew shadow on substance. He loved photographing bedsteads, scrawny porch furniture, fences and grates, because they tattooed matter. The emotional register in the sharecropper pictures is intense but narrow, since their effects are so exclusively determined by moral selectivity and reformist impulse. (We see the same narrowness in Lewis Hine, and for the same reasons.) Frank's pictures ranged across class and racial lines, landscapes, social groups, public and private events, and ceremonies. The tones are more mixed and vexing. Frank saw more in his viewfinder than Evans did, I think, or at least allowed a wider possibility for what's given. Evans's pictures have an evangelical force and memorialize a particular kind of hunger and want in its historical setting, but Frank possessed a more innocent, inquiring, merciful eye.

Evans used the camera to scan, without interpreting, the sign language that cultures generate, signage that's for all intents and purposes authorless, which materializes through a kind of parthenogenesis. The movie announcements he photographed during his trip to Cuba in 1933 rush out at us, each plaintive in its own way. Though he was politically sensitive, it's unlikely Evans realized how prescient the placard for *Six Hours to Live* would be: the corrupt presidency of Gerardo Machado collapsed just after Evans left. Movie posters hold a sexual charge that other signage doesn't. They edit life at a high pitch. Their lettering looks suddenly aroused, blatant, auspicious, bearing all the urgencies of pleasure and abandonment. They come on to us. Evans's pictures of public lettering bear his emotional signature: bemused aloofness and cruel alertness. He had a good eye for language in the making, or unmaking. And yet while he had a gift for imaging the disordering power of poster art and signage, there's no erotic charge between his camera and its subject, all the more apparent when the subject isn't signage but a beautiful young *cubana* in tight-fitting pumps. What suffices? A cigar, a uniform, shoes, a Panama hat? A chair, a tin can or pot, a desirable body, carfare? Evans's eye seems casually to fall upon such things and just as casually shade them with political consequence. Unlike images produced by other scrutinizers of the different poverties a society generates and allows—Dorothea Lange, Roy Stryker, Russell Lee—Evans's pictures are moodless. He's our most pitiless photographer, Shakeresque in his pictorial economies, no matter how busy the scene, especially when treating extremities of abundance or destitution. The little that suffices is never really enough. Not even everything suffices.

✡

When after many years I saw again a large print of Frank's "U.S. 66, Arizona," it felt like an image that had entered my dream life, shockingly familiar yet unaccommodated, something fled from memory now vividly restored. Photographic images hit us hard because they're printed directly from nature. They jump onto our nerves. "U.S. 66, Arizona" looks now like an "imitation" of O'Sullivan's Gettysburg picture, though the awfulness in Frank's image—a highway traffic accident—broods in the folds of the blanket covering victims stretched across the broad central foreground. Behind them stand five people, each angled differently toward the corpses, each attitude a ceremonialism of feeling. They stare at the blanket. Buildings in the background span frontier history: 1950s ranch house; a garage; a squatter, older, makeshift house; an outhouse; and a tumbledown wooden shack. But it's all one action of life and death. Like the standing witnesses, like the telephone wires that faintly skim the horizon, those structures are snowed over by wooly flecks, like windblown chaff or weed dust, that not only come to rest in the solid stuff of the blanket covering the corpses but also swarm from it.

✡

Fox Talbot said that his china cabinet calotype was better than a written inventory, for if the collection were stolen the picture would be "mute testimony" to its reality, "evidence of a novel kind," a record of an existence. A little later in the century, the public equivalent of such witness was Atget's grand project of photographing the old and new Paris. Once the cabinet's contents leave their niche, their household museum, they become commodities whose assigned values can be documented. Atget made photography a witness and transcriber of the commodity life of objects. Many of the ten thousand pictures he took were of the new Paris created by Baron Haussmann, Napoleon III's prefect of the Seine. By 1870, one-fifth of Paris's streets were Haussmann's creation; more than a quarter million of the city's poorer inhabitants had been displaced by the destruction of old buildings. A new economic order was emerging. The manufacture and merchandising of objects were centralized; large-scale suppliers assembled goods speedily for large retail outlets. The change was mounted and displayed in the windows of the *grands magasins* which by 1870 had created their own "views" for Parisians to study and absorb. Those frames presented and enclosed objects of desire. Spend too long looking at Atget's shop-front pictures thronged with blouses, shoes, petticoats, corsets, trousers, hats, gloves, and shawls, and you'll get department store vertigo (or nausea).

Atget's act of witness is more complex than his predecessors could have imagined, because of the mediating quality of the shop window, its squinting view of commerce. The glass that clarifies objects of desire also reflects images of the social matrix outside. In many of the pictures, the street scene swims in the middle distance of the glass. We see the objects of desire and their "support," where the stones of Haussmann's Paris lie imprinted on the image of the new, shared, public life of desire. But it's a glass support. Atget was dramatizing the transparency of prohibition when we confront things we desire. His pictures testified to the new system of dependencies, of plenitudes and deprivations. The prosperity that ignites and sustains desire is pinched by images he made in 1912 of plump, overdressed prostitutes outside their cribs, and of the mean shanties of the *chiffonniers* and the coach-cart dwellings of *zoniers*, populations literally marginalized, pushed to the city's outskirts, by Haussmann's demolitions and by the new wealth driving up rents. Atget's encyclopedist zeal resulted in a photo-history of the economic processes implicit in free-market prosperity. I don't mean his images are illustrational. They represent stress patterns the photographer saw as he spent those many years moving literally from the old Paris to the new, corner by corner, quarter by quarter. It helps to see images like "Bitumiers" and "Paveurs," the badly paid work gangs wreathed in vapor who paved the way for the new century's automobiles—Haussmann's urban renewal made fast fortunes for manufacturers of tar macadam—in proximity with an image like "Boutique automobile, avenue de la Grande Armée," taken in 1924. Behind the welcoming glass façade stands a new car, broadside, its spare hanging from a fender like an earring; two other models face parade-front. The cars are already museum spooks rendered nearly transparent in the glass's glare.

Photography delivers—sometimes more piercingly than we're prepared for—the solid presentness of material civilization as memorial to itself. When a photograph recalls material reality, it also delivers its immaterial wraith or larva. Atget's "Boutique automobile" image implicates not only the vehicles on display but also the pavers and street workers and steelworkers, and the glazier, and the sign painter, whose newly created job was to enhance the glazier's work by naming the new objects of desire and who did so in the hope that he too might enter the cycle, obtain such an object, enlist his energies in that system of dependencies. The image is particularly disturbing because in the window, on the support, are reflected the sidewalk trees. In the spectral depths of the treetops where they diminish toward a point deep in the image, we see autumnal decay, the sparse leafage and branches that seem to grow into and through those lovely, gawky machines.

✡

Why the erotic pinch of photographs? A picture, like love or mania, expresses fanatical attention. Maybe because the whole shape of the ghost of the flesh is already there, and yet not there, I mean not *here,* not actual (the image tells us that, too), its likeness so like what we imagine our own likeness to be. We see ourselves remembered, already posthumous, sometimes smiling. In a studio portrait of my grandmother as a young woman in Abruzzo, I see the dignified stillness and compassionate self-containment men found so attractive. In a snapshot of my father, taken in South Philadelphia in his early twenties, I see the familiar shadow structure and stress lines of my own face. A third image, of my grandmother and grandfather, not long after she crossed over to join him in South Philadelphia: my young grandfather, who would die a few months later, has the alert, wolfish features of my father in that other picture. My grandmother wears a dark, simple dress and high-laced boots. They're both dressed in too frequently brushed and washed and ironed grays and whites. Their faces wear the strained look of what Henry James called the launched populations. But now, in my life of looking at pictures, other presences sharpen the pinch of those family snapshots even more. Lewis Hine, Walker Evans, Paul Strand—they are there, too.

✡

The image existence of a black-and-white photo is obtained by exiling matter's primary visual quality: color. A photo doesn't so much copy its subject as it takes an imprint of its sketchwork. When we see a news picture showing us the death of the body, the pathos is piercing but forgettable: although we recognize at once the exact "print" of the event, of death's actuality, the signs of the life of the flesh have already fled from the image. And we remember historical events in black-and-white images. Their archival accuracy surpasses that of paintings, coins, graphics, tapestries. Photography processes magnitudes and multitudes. Yet, like those other forms, it's become conventionalized as representation merely. The historical imagination, the way consciousness represents past reality to itself, absorbs these new abstractions quickly. What if pictures of the death camps, of Hiroshima and Nagasaki, preserved the look of color-drenched flesh or flesh from which the flush of life has been drained? How would that affect our recognition and memory of horror? Did the documentation in color photographs of the Vietnam War make our consciousness of that bloodshed different from that of previous wars? In 1857, when sepia images were the norm, the Goncourt brothers (who sat for a portrait by Nadar) declared: "Everything is becoming black in this century; photographs are the black clothing of things." Black-and-white's ceremonialism has become so central and commonplace in our lives that we accept in pictures what our imagination unassisted would resist. Black leaves, black water, black roses. Or the reverse. In Minor White's visionary landscapes trees are solarized to cotton-wool white, not as if they lacked or wanted color, but as if all color had rushed to those green lives with such force and concentration as to vaporize them. And yet, black-and-white photography can powerfully reveal the shaping streams around the human figure. Like Frank, Paul Strand did his best work when he was a stranger to the place. He liked to use the framing rhetoric of windows, doors, and gates to increase the pressure created by the selective housing of the viewfinder. In "The Family" (Luzzara, Italy, 1953) impoverishments fold out beyond the definitions of the funereal door frame: the gazes of a mother and her five grown sons (barefoot, their trouser legs rolled up) are cast in different directions. Each gaze—defiant, wistful, confused, surrendering—expresses a different way of absorbing circumstance. They look rooted there but not trapped—it's the frame of material necessity that holds them. Their faces register nothing migratory or expectant. Like other straight photographers, Strand lives in the country of the seeable, of what's merely given, and what he sees is the substance of flesh in the stream of its place. But that's part of the natural history of photography: the pang we feel looking at snapshots of dead loved ones is due to that rush of presentness, of seeing a grandparent or father in the world-stream while we're hostage to the knowledge that the person has disappeared.

✿

Every great city has its own central nervous system. Good street photographers make it visible. Walker Evans's New York is cool, taut, and secretive. Robert Frank's is wobbly, melancholy, ambiguous. Louis Faurer (a friend of Frank's and 1950s colleague on the staff of *Harper's Bazaar*) started making photographs in South Philadelphia only a few blocks from where I was raised: in cities his eye was drawn toward prosperity burred against trauma, eccentricity, and destitution. He loved Market Street's focused mania. "Whatever you saw passing by," he said, "could be photographed." In one picture, a black amputee beggar is visible through the legs of a store-window manikin. We're in Atget-land. The window surface projects the store's interior muddled by the reflection of a Horn and Hardart automat across the street. New York changed Faurer's style, or he changed his style to find *it*. The Philadelphia pictures are fully, diffusely lit, but it's a daytime moodiness. In New York Faurer began doing nocturnes that are among the best night photos we have. Times Square's incandescent lights were for him the equivalent of a painter's drapery. He could dress a scene with them, use them as framing or balancing components, play up their excitability. He pushed the medium hard, using very slow film in underlit situations, so that light looks like fluid squeezed from its black surround. In a picture of two kids leaning over a match to light cigarettes, the match tip's disk of shattered light repeats along a string of double-exposed streetlights rolling into the background. It's as if the kids hold the city's life-giving fire in their hands.

✿

Photography creates intimacies and costumes reality. Seeing a snapshot of someone, anyone, tempts us to believe we know that person, because we count on the candor of the medium, until we remember that a fictitious self can be contrived for the occasion. Photographers are attracted by whatever's secretive, out of place, or freakish. Diane Arbus said: "A photograph is a secret about a secret. The more it tells you the less you know." A picture says: Come out, come out, wherever you are. What's given to the camera, even the personality of a loved one, is mysterious. A photo's illusionism throws an opaque sheath or membrane around the subject, glazing a truth we want to believe exists. Arbus's subjects—the Jewish giant whose head grazes the ceiling; the transvestite whose look says come hither, darling, come on, I dare you; mental patients cavorting in a darkling Halloweenish nowhere land; children in a ballroom dancing contest dressed like large dolls—have a depressive flamboyance cuffed by an emotional restraint that keeps them just this side of exploitation. Her pictures bear an implicit directive: Behold But Do Not Judge. Their intimacy instills a creepy suspicion that we're looking at versions of ourselves, that like her we're all oddities of a kind. Loaded content, for sure, and yet an Arbus image offers hardly any formal excitement. Her images can bring us down, not because of the afflictions and melancholy on display but because of their dim, deteriorated, rubbed-raw settings. These weren't accidental. Arbus did much of her own printing. Her deliberateness is most acute in the penumbral lighting that traps "the retarded people" she photographed in 1970–71. Her work, obsessed as it is with the self-as-décor, is closest not to the modern tradition but to early medical photography and to the fashion photography that paid her rent.

✡

Fashion photography is all migratory, a readiness to escape necessity or pretend it doesn't exist. Richard Avedon's images quiver with the anxiety to flee the material present toward a future, any future. His subjects lack a world-stream. The shaping forces, as in Diane Arbus's work, are internal, eruptive, florid. In her extreme close-up "A Young Man in Curlers at Home on West Twentieth Street, N.Y.C., 1966," we see plucked stubble beneath the skinny black gull's wings of the young man's penciled eyebrows. An identity is being coaxed into being; the man is "at home" in the self he's designing, since there's not much material context in the picture. In "Tattooed Man at a Carnival, Md., 1970," the matted filaments of hair on the man's chest and abdomen look like they've sprouted from the animal and bird tattoos there. And the tattoos look like they've bloomed from his blood or developed slowly in a solution like a photograph. These kinds of images borrow from fashion photography the primacy of arranged or carefully determined contexts. The human subject is selected because it's "dressed," as a movie set is "dressed." The figure volatilizes all suggestion of necessity so that it can stand as something triumphantly singular, free of contingency. It's a pure expression of irreligion—it can't allow for any suggestion of the human emerging from something greater (or more inclusive) than itself. In its skittish present, the fashion figure colonizes everything around it. Consider Avedon's image of a slaughterhouse worker from *In the American West*, an instance of working-class photography like Hine's made over into fashion photography. A wiry Asian or American Indian figure in a spattered apron strikes the familiar Avedon pose, confrontational yet disengaged, a pigsticker and other tools hanging from his belt. He's embellished, dressed, with the bloody residues of his job, but against the white backdrop he has no context to stream him into the nature of his work. He's exiled, history-less, abstract. The title, "Blue Cloud Wright" (his name), suggesting a long, troubled, and maybe deeply religious racial history, is a smug enhancement: the irony sits on the picture waiting for some intelligible, enlivening context. But the picture's real purpose lies in that pigsticker, the tattoos, the leather apron, the gore dripping from the subject's fingertips: all have the singularized, fragmentary insularity of belts, earrings, shoes, or watches in a fashion spread.

✡

The workers in the depressed smokestack towns of Ohio and Pennsylvania that Lee Friedlander photographed in 1979–80 for *Factory Valleys* possess a somnolent patience. A welder slouches nonchalantly across his workbench: wearing a slit-eye mask and gray coveralls, he looks like a postindustrial gnome or miner-dwarf, a completely subterranean creature whose torch shoots brief white acetylene wings. Another image: a man and woman stand with numbed watchfulness behind a drop forge's square iron mouth, arms raised in a ritualized, almost matrimonial, gesture. Though framed by the machine's aperture, nothing suggests they're trapped or captive; their look is one of effortless disinterestedness, neither crushed nor redeemed by work. This side of the forge lies a glittering puzzle of identical punched-out slugs.

Friedlander depicts workers as absorbed in their labor but aware that its uniform products pass beyond them. The system of material relations—the interdependence of worker, machine, and product, an extension of the new capital that Atget documented—is quietly stated, while crucial discriminations are held intact: the workers aren't automatons, and their activity isn't represented as grindingly reductive or demeaning. In the racial and sexual variety of workers at various tasks we see a form of human industry now practically vanished from the American economy. These laborers are doing the work of a civilization, but the world context—the messy, underpopulated shops where the work gets done—is changing faster than they can know. Friedlander's welders, wire rollers, small-parts assemblers, and all the rest are trying to hold their place in an economy's debris. The answering images in the series are the weedy, desolate autumnal and wintry landscapes of those towns, where even the natural order looks like scrap that must be either collected or allowed to rust away.

THUNDERBALL

In one of my favorite movie scenes in Hitchcock's *Sabotage*, his adaptation of Conrad's *The Secret Agent*, a Scotland Yard inspector, investigating a cell of conspirators in wartime London, walks down the side aisle of the Bijou Cinema, owned by Mr. Verloc, who lives with his family on the premises. We track the agent as he moves, catching his slant view of the screen, its twitchy shadows and lights, the audience rapt and laughing. He then sneaks behind the screen to eavesdrop on the saboteurs meeting in Verloc's lodgings. When he inserts himself behind the illusion, the image we saw moments ago projected on the front of the screen we now see looming on the verso, gross and tissuey and hyperbolic. Its power to control group emotion, to improvise a mob, seems all the more grotesque and scary when we see the massive wafered image close-up, depthless and wraithlike. We hear what the inspector hears. On one side, the vivid social life of image fiction—the projector's throaty roll, the audience's rustling amazement; on the other, voices which have the power to bring death to innocents. (Later, the young brother of Verloc's wife, unknowingly transporting a terrorist time bomb to Piccadilly Circus along with film reels of *Bartholomew the Strangler*, is killed when the bomb goes off in a crowded, slow-moving bus.) The cozy preserve of the movie house rumbles happily just a few steps from the kind of terrorist intent that can turn a Bijou into a shambles.

✿

From when I was a kid, spending weekends at double features, I've loved movie houses for their shared secrecy, anonymous company, and unmenacing spookiness. Even in an overlit suburban multiplex, I feel the same queasy anticipation before the big screen that awaits its images. Whenever I've moved, I've always made an early visit to the local movie house to get the feel of the place and eavesdrop on the conversation up there on screen. Testifying to big manipulative moving images in a big dark room feels like the first stage of local citizenship. The drama of moviegoing is inseparable from our sense of "the movies." Around the narrative of the picture we wrap narratives of our presence or degree of involvement or the stage of our lives. How intimate is it? A woman over thirty years ago pulled close to me in one of San Francisco's then-plentiful single-screen theaters and hooked her arm through mine in a way that promised later the most wowing sex we would ever have, at a French detective picture, *Without Apparent Motive*, starring one of my favorite actors, Jean-Louis Trintignant—he's right up there with Gian Maria Volontè and Marcello—performing an homage to Bogart, his snarly grin directed mostly at Dominique Sanda's big-cat slinkiness. Jean-Louis wore gray slacks, navy blazer, and dark knit tie. A few days later, after that night's sex, I bought myself such an outfit.

✡

We contain moviegoing, absorb it, in a candid, social, often urgent, close-up, shareable way. In the early 1970s, at the old Telegraph Repertory in Berkeley, a showing of Sam Peckinpah's *The Wild Bunch*, the most violent movie of the time, whose moral complexity consisted of the outlaws' response to certain death—"Why not?"—was followed by riotous cries of "Fascist bullshit!" Other voices shouted "This is real American art!" *The Wild Bunch* existed in three different lengths, each with different amounts of backstory. I'd already seen the most complete version of it at the Embassy in San Francisco, an exquisitely decrepit and now defunct Market Street movie palace that sometimes showed offbeat stuff that appealed to serious fans and that doubled as a relatively safe flophouse for winos, druggies, and transients like me, where we all got to participate in the "Big Wheel!" contest spin that interrupted evening shows. A few nights after the Berkeley showing, I was waiting to squeeze into a small auditorium to see a clandestine print of the then-sequestered *Titicut Follies*, while a young man behind me talked thrillingly about finally getting to see that coolly hellish documentary about conditions in a state-operated insane asylum. But along with that, he speed-babbled some anecdote about Callas singing *Tosca*, bits of which he explosively sang (in beautiful Italian) while nattering about the forbidden document we were all about to see.

✡

Multiplexes got started a long time ago, but they weren't the sort we have now. The 1970s prototypes were art houses carved up into multiple viewing chambers to accommodate more independent and foreign pictures, or to show mainstream movies that would offset the expense of showing less conventional fare. Culture atrophies if it doesn't change, and change brings the pangs or pains of the unfamiliar shoving aside what's known and rosy. In the early 1990s I lived in Redwood City, a suburb south of San Francisco, and tried not to get cranky when features at my local multiplex were projected on a curved screen designed to accommodate the satellite-pod viewing rooms spoked around a huge central lobby that functioned as a combined mess hall and video arcade. This particular multiplex was constructed on a strip of land between a freeway and marshy bay shore, mushroomed there at land's end, in an enormous parking lot along a row of car dealerships and unfinished-furniture outlets, about one mile from Redwood City's small, listless downtown. It was called an "Entertainment Center," though it wasn't the center of anything. While its ambience and offerings adapted to (and shaped) suburban habits, it kept at least one traditional social function. It was a place where you knew you could always find people. And so one summer when angry teenagers from one of our neighborhoods wanted to find the boy they felt had "dissed" them, they drove by the multiplex at 1 P.M. of a sunny Sunday and fired into the available teenage crowd. One adaptation of the suburban multiplex is to have made itself, by virtue of its physical isolation, a good shooting gallery. Inside the center are video games imaging mock firepower of very imaginative kinds, and beyond these are the cinemas themselves. On their screens, behind which lie no spaces for investigators or saboteurs, guns of the most ingenious designs are being gleefully fired at all shapes and sizes of human beings, and at mock humans, too, at holographic and androidal and virtually real human beings, and at molten humanoids that can revivify themselves so that they may be shot again.

✡

Megadeath movies—and Westerns, thrillers, disaster movies, and gang-culture pictures—cheer (while sentimentally chastising) the power over creation that guns allow. It's an American theme. Killing and entitlement get married. The Judge in Cormac McCarthy's *Blood Meridian* gives voice to it. Educated, polyglot, knowledgeable of the names and natural histories of things, the seven-foot-tall, chalky white, hairless cowboy is the best-informed killer of a gang of scalp hunters roaming Mexico in the 1840s. The Judge's morality tolerates only what exists by his sanction: "Whatever exists, whatever in creation exists without my knowledge exists without my consent. In order for the earth to be mine nothing must be permitted to occur upon it save by my dispensation." That's the decree of a God with a gun. It's the dispensation of murderousness. For all the "compassion" (lucky us) in megadeath movies, they're finally illustrations of the Judge's mind. Control through killing. In Homer, the word for "work," *ergon,* is used to describe what men do in battle—the work of killing. The Judge's dispensation is the power that audiences cheer and applaud.

✡

Motion picture images are invasive of consciousness in ways that paintings, photographs, and lines of poetry are not. These are subversive and insinuating—they imitate reality by transfiguring it. Motion picture images don't imitate appearances, they replicate them with an excruciating intensity and saturatedness. (How we learn to tolerate those intensities in our private and social lives is another matter.) They are a superfluity, reiterating or repronouncing the world visually with such concentrated energy and retinal suddenness that they cut into consciousness as poems and pictures do not. Movie images can be more repulsive, smothering, executive, or totalitarian in the way they determine the feeling tones of physical reality. They leave us feeling violated or rescued or elated, but they don't have the moral consequence that poetry has. Poetry critically influences the way we deliberate on and differentiate among the particulars of the world. Movies offer globalizing feeling, not the severe hyperattentiveness to nuance and degree we get from lines of verse or from good painting. And yet certain moments in movies, while giving up nothing of that invasive power, have in them a kind of poetry. I'm thinking of compositions or sequences that fill consciousness with knowledge of mortality—comic, violent, obscene, melodramatic, whatever the tone—and make of such knowledge a gaiety. I mean the gaiety or joy of consciousness that poetry can give. The quiet swordsman shot during the battle against the brigands in *The Seven Samurai* falls as warriors since antiquity are said to "fall," with a fated weightedness and gravity, like Homer's princes who fall from their chariots and their armor clatters upon them and darkness closes over their eyes. The samurai falls and the muddy rainwater churns around him. At the end of *Children of Paradise* Baptiste plunges helplessly through the crowd of carnival revelers to reach and call back his beloved Garance, who disappears in that sea. He is tossed and held back by the tide of celebrants all dressed like his theatrical self, Pierrot. His own stage image becomes an indiscriminate mass that prevents him from reclaiming his lover. Marcello, in the last scene of *The Conformist,* sits in the street crib of a Roman male prostitute, having just learned that the man he thought he accidentally killed when he was a boy (which crime he thought to expiate by becoming a Fascist collaborator and assassin) is still alive. He turns and looks over his shoulder. Behind him a fire burns. It's a Platonic turn, the turn of the prisoners in the cave, away from the shadows cast by the firelight on the wall of the cave, to look beyond the fire to the reality it illuminates. It's a moment of political and moral recognition when agonized private conscience is suddenly jarred into relation with history. Then there is the comic moment in *Rear Window* when Grace Kelly, surprised by Raymond Burr as she searches his apartment for evidence of his wife's murder, wiggles her finger behind her back so that James Stewart (who loves Kelly but is reluctant to marry), viewing the scene from his window across the courtyard, can see the wedding band, the evidence of the lost wife. In that instant, Burr notices her surreptitious gesture, follows the line of sight, and sees the investigator-voyeur across the way. The triangulated moment of moral implication and comic mock marriage binds all three characters in a compact of guilty knowledge.

✡

Certain scenes arc over and *through* my life with a speed and suddenness that imitate the medium itself, which rips through the meditative delay, the pause rationality requires, that other art forms depend on. In Walter Hill's *Wild Bill,* a sullen, rueful meditation on the life of Bill Hickok (played with wistful, killer-angel sweetness by Jeff Bridges), an avenger (Bruce Dern) in a wheel-chair rolls into the dust-gagged street and hollers to our hero, who's relaxing (and trying to avoid situations just like this one) in a saloon: "I'm calling you out, Wild Bill!" It's high school, inner city, circa 1962. I'm shuffling down the two-way traffic hall between classes and some brute in a sharkskin suit—dress codes ruled in diocesan schools in those days, and certain South Philly boys, like guys in *Mean Streets* and *Goodfellas,* were murderous *and* dandified—steps out of the opposing flow of traffic, bumps me hard, and says: "Hey, faggot, I'm calling you out." But who is he? And why is he doing this? Don't ask. My culture's answer was: "It is what it is, deal with it." I'm amused by fans of movie and TV versions of Italian American culture who, having grown up in perfectly civil households and neighborhoods where the word "reason" is sometimes spoken, express grudging admiration for the crazed, volcanic violence of word and deed in Martin Scorsese pictures and *The Sopranos.* (Oh, how often murderous paternal Tony says "It is what it is" because it's evidence of some irreducible code of conduct without moral ambiguity or relativism, a purified animalism chagrined and appalled by psychotherapeutic interfer-ence.) You always know where you stand. Fuck reason. Sometimes you have to slap around loved ones for their own good, no? Honor and self-respect are large. Except when they're not. A prank we boys played stood for a general rule of conduct. You light a cigarette and tell a friend: "Press my chest when I inhale and you'll see smoke come out my ears." While he presses and watches your ears, you screw the fag's red bud into the back of his hand. By the time he registers pain, addled by shock and humiliation, you've made your mark. So you punch him in the stomach, he whooshes, drops to the pavement. He's sucking air and trying to grok what's wrong with his hand. You pull him up and give him a little hug. "Hey, man, you're okay." Ask me no question and I'll tell you no lies. Wild Bill, who years before cuckolded the Dern char-acter, sighing and grimacing as if his past is a *thing* he keeps banging his shins against, goes outside and shoots the wheelchair gunslinger dead.

✡

Before high school and its surprising corridors, I spent Saturday afternoons at double features. It gave me a tingle to approach the President Theater on Snyder Avenue (still standing in South Philadelphia, though now used by a catering business), where the twin bill would be Mummy movies, Randolph

Scott horse operas, *King Kong* teamed with *Mighty Joe Young* ("Beautiful dreamer, how I love you!"), or Martin and Lewis comedies. The splashy rotogravure posters, like the gaudy carnival fliers stapled to telephone poles in summer, were a smash of colors rarely seen in our houses. Their sexy, trouncing energy promised an intensified life inside. I followed the opening credits to prolong my anticipation of the crepuscular dimming of house lights. In the lobby, the candy counter glowed in the dark like a cherry red El Dorado Biarritz in a showroom or a hi-fi console at a make-out party. I don't like the lobby casino lighting in our multiplexes. Not much sexy promise there, though I still check out credits of coming attractions, especially if the picture stars Jeff Bridges or Johnny Depp.

✿

A disturbing moment of desire in Steven Soderbergh's *The Limey*. The thuggish ex-con played by Terence Stamp visits L.A. to find out how his daughter died and who was responsible. Classic tough guy, Stamp moves forward, always forward, like a force of nature, shooting people, throwing not-as-tough guys off bridges, insisting on answers. The desire strikes when moments from his earlier life, with his wife and daughter, spike into his consciousness. But they aren't traditionally framed flashbacks: the scenes he recalls are those he actually lived, since the flashbacks are from *Poor Cow*, the sixties movie where a young, angelic Terence Stamp plays a petty thief. The immediacy of the recall is sick-making, so rich in what-if possibility is the vision of a life lived before choices were made, choices that would lead to the death of the grown-up flashback child that the old man is now trying to solve. Replay-life: words represent the deliberative process of recovery and its affects. Movie imagery lives it out for us, a proxy for consciousness, with all the sensuous immediacy of hurt and loss. Movies make such sluts of us, sluts for the recovery of earlier selves, of a forked road we've already put behind. And we reflect on our earlier moments as if they were film stills, not motion pictures. We live the continuity but reflect on the stilled container of experience.

✿

Living in Italy in the early 1970s, I spent the better part of one afternoon seeking a remote movie house in suburban Florence showing Sergio Leone's

Once Upon a Time in the West. I'd seen his early pictures with their peculiar casts—the great Italian political actor Gian Maria Volontè co-starred in *For a Few Dollars More* and *A Fistful of Dollars*—but what put me to the trouble of tracking down his latest was the movie poster I'd seen somewhere. On a train platform, in the middle of a dusty prairie, gunslingers are blazing away. In the foreground, nearest us, a six-shooter flies from the hand of a cowboy just shot, now suspended midair in a Fosbury flop. The others assume classic *contrapposto* positions, twisting one way or another. It's a barren place where very little suffices and guns rule.

✡

Whenever I went to the movies in Italy, whether a deluxe theater or *cinema parrocchiale* (a movie house attached to a church), I paused to study the movie cards. Great ones, like those for Bertolucci's *The Conformist* and *Last Tango in Paris* or Visconti's *Ludwig*, were concentrates of stylistic feeling. As I often did at the President, I peeked inside before entering, to prime myself for its melodramatic charms. My favorites were the parochial houses with their linoleum flooring, hard chairs, grayish screen, slightly louche parishioners peddling cigarettes and candy bars at intermission, and the bingo hall lighting which *dropped* to total darkness before the screen fizzed into life. The posters, ambience, and usually inauspicious programming are for me inseparable from language, since I used to drop in, often three or four times a week, at the *cinema parrocchiale* of the Church of San Martino—its piazza served as a parking lot on weekdays; you experienced its piazza-ness only on Sundays—to practice Italian. Bad movies badly dubbed are a good occasion for learning idioms, so I sat there repeating aloud phrases that caught my ear. Once, I became aware of something squirming next to me. I turned and saw a young boy climbing over armrests back to his mother, whispering (as one does in church), "Mamma mamma! È pazzo quello lí!" Mama, that guy's crazy! And so I was, in a moviegoing way. The Church of San Martino also offered sustenance and respite. Bologna's summers are so infernal that evening shows were projected outdoors, late, on a huge screen mounted on the upper story of the church's inner courtyard, the cloister, a place of solitude and meditation, where for centuries priests prayed, counseled agonized parishioners, whispered devotions from their breviaries, and where one night I watched, with a huge crowd, *Thunderball*.

NICE TOUCH

One of the tenderest gestures in movies happens in *On the Waterfront* when Eva Marie Saint lifts her hand to caress Marlon Brando's face, laying it against his temple and cheek as if to contain the melancholy confusion and rage fired up in his conscience. Her impulsive touch is meant to becalm and protect, but also to give momentary shape to the disorder inside his head and lay its destructive passion to rest. Touch is the most casual gesture, and yet even when casual or unthinking it can carry a sparky charge of hope or desire. It can tear apart or complete a bond. We put our hand over another's to restrain or console, to bestow, to claim or own. A mother presses her palm to a child's forehead as an instinctual shielding caress and as a talismanic gesture that might drain a fever from the child's body and run it through her own. When we're fatigued our own hand propping up the head feels like someone else's touch, or like a useful, unfamiliar object. A woman fanning her fingers to tip up another woman's chin turns that little space they occupy into a theatrical zone where display is life's most concentrated critical action and glittering affection is inseparable from wicked exposure. A sculptor friend tells me that when working she feels constantly that the things around her want to be touched, not just the materials but also the forms coming into existence—her laying-on of hands is an answering form-giving gesture. The sensation of surfaces like glass, stone, or wood can make us feel mysteriously more complete as material beings. Specific objects—handbags, coins, canes, bottles—feel as if they want to come into fresh forms, forms of use, and the way we hold and handle them becomes part of our personality's signature. A scramble of friends folded and linked across a floor compose a neighborhood of flesh wherein every body draws a sense of safety and sanctuary from the closed circuit of physical connections. Dance and your partner's flesh and bone feel so feathery that you thrill to the touch of such live weight. Lift or move a dead person and at your touch the body feels too heavy for what's there, for what's left.

THIS THING

The mind freights weather with its own confabulations and anxieties. Serial rainstorms here in San Francisco, intermittent blue mist—the Asian mist of hillside screen paintings—infiltrating trees in Golden Gate Park. The lull between storms softens things. The rain starts up again like cat-o'-nine tails thrashing my windows. A certain kind of depression, my kind—a Motownish lyric there: "My kind, my kind, my kind"—brings episodes that beat against the coastline of the sane or balanced self, baffled by meds and the talking cure. It's not curable because it's the *nature* of that particular self. (Or, in my own mental menagerie: the dragon of chaos must be fed, else he rip apart every order he sees; he never goes away; he sleeps in the gate.) Late one night, writing, I start to break up (who knows why? Unknowability is pain's core; sobbing is the stupefied noise pain makes) and so lie on the floor waiting for the waves, the dragonish sea, the unnameable hurt, to pass over.

✪

This thing of darkness I / Acknowledge mine.
—Prospero speaking of Caliban

Takes one to know one. The eighteenth-century poet William Cowper cannily and amicably conceals his secret suicidal melancholia in the flowering shrubs of his letters, which craft a wholesome, amiable personality, but he admits to "[putting] on an air of cheerfulness and vivacity to which I am in reality a stranger." It was "the arduous task of being merry by force. Despair made amusements necessary, and I found poetry the most agreeable amusement." He lived with the unwanted companion and made himself a good one. His pain, his madness, was the raised rough grain of his sense of failure in belief, in life as devotion. To feel unworthy of God is, in derangement, to be convinced of being unworthy of life.

✡

Most days, writing takes on the emotional lucidity of dream life, its bite and garish clarity, but it's also bereavement, tracing or tracking what's no longer among us. The more you write, the more you feel something is missing, will always be missing; that ache makes you want to write more, inviting more of the same. So bereavement is a kind of grotesque bounty. Some mornings, gulping the oxygen of waking life out of a dream's suffocation, I feel bereft, though I can't remember what exactly has been lost, other than the dream state I wanted to escape; I can't remember any shape of face or body, just an ectoplasmic force, the spirit of the human presence in the dream now transformed into a felt compulsion. Write it down, then. Write it out. But not out of your system. Getting older, I don't so much want to remember things in poetry. I want to *keep* them.

✡

That life is lived between God and derangement? Fall from one, fall into the other?

✡

Clinical melancholia doesn't color one's feeling for reality, it determines it. The fall of light, a child's laughter, a lover's whisper, wind unsettling curtains, a towhee hopping on gravel—every moment is fraught with fatefulness. The most delicate things become fatty deposits of the worst-is-yet-to-come. Flight, the sight of it, induces the agony of impossibility: a gull oaring itself into the air makes you weep because it's a grandiose vision of the impossible. Gravity rules. It defines you, and you are null. The bed is the best and worst place. It's the island where you're safe, if not from the serrated confabulations of your own consciousness, then at least from afflictions that the world beyond the bed will, you're certain, bring you. It's the worst place because the longer you're there, the more it loves you, the more it renews its sticky torpor. It's a safe place to consider killing yourself.

✡

"People have reason to be depressed beyond their neurotransmitters" (Glen Gabbard, Menninger Clinic psychiatrist). Weltschmerz. There should be a single word in English for that. If we're awake to the fact that human action is a way of serving a dream of existence, we're liable to feel an overpowering helplessness and irrelevance—the irrelevance of everything, a suicidal irrelevance—and its physical expression is cryptic silence and self-removal. (Cue sobs here.) It's systemic, a toxin in the circulatory system of spirit. You don't contract it, it *comes for you,* genetically and in the world—it weaves its tacky filaments into your temperament. When in melancholia, the body wakes from dreams feeling like a gummy slab, as if the effort of dreaming depletes the soul's energy to rise.

YOUR SHOW OF SHOWS

In 1968, in a windowless cinder-block dressing room of a small college theater on Philadelphia's Main Line, I saw Sid Caesar in his skivvies and full-calf black socks, listing on one leg while he tried to smooth his hose. Two handlers stood by. The occasion was the opening of a new theater at St. Joseph's College, where I went to school and earned money crewing for events. It was no small thing, seeing in the flesh the man I'd known from 1950s television. I loved *Your Show of Shows* and, later, *Caesar's Hour*. One of his best routines was playing the dizzy, disheveled Professor Von Houdinoff, expert on magicians, who wore a mashed top hat and held a chewed-up cigar butt. The skits with his partner, the great horsy-faced comedienne Imogene Coca, were so funny and inventive that I fed off them for days. The shows were live, so you never knew what might happen. The scripts were worked out enough to seem stable, but the medium itself made them combustible. As a comic presence, Sid Caesar was my long-suffering Dauphin of Heebie-Jeebies, his body a wincing, slightly aggrieved shape of energy. Then there was his laugh. No great comic has a straightforward laugh. (Think of Art Carney, Milton Berle, Richard Pryor, Bill Murray.) Sid Caesar's was squirmy, fragile, and hilariously pitiable. Television had made him one of the richest men in show business; by the age of thirty he was earning a million a year. So why was this brilliant entertainer performing in such a punk venue? At first I hardly recognized him. His skin sagged and was so thinned-out that the face looked inadequately fitted to the bones. In 1982, when he published his autobiography *Where Have I Been*, I learned

163

that the Philadelphia gig happened during his lost years. He was by then so far gone on Equanil and Seconal (in the A.M.) and booze (from noon on) that he was drunk or stoned practically all day every day. The serious drinking started when *Caesar's Hour* was canceled in 1958. He hit bottom in 1978 and decided to dry out. So he went to Canada! Finally clean and sober, he couldn't remember much of what had happened. Big chunks of time, years on end, were erased. Once in a while a fact would float by. About going to Australia in 1975 to do a movie called *Barnaby and Me,* he said: "I don't remember anything about the trip or picture. I lost a whole continent." Memory is so opportunistic. Sid Caesar was just a hoot and a dream image when I was a kid, but over the years he somehow became in my imagination an all-purpose image of comedic play, *homo ludens* American-style, pinched by self-consciousness. Balancing on one leg in that dressing room, he was someone else. Seeing him in the flesh, I lost him, lost at least my mental image of him. Irrational and self-serving as it was, I felt a vague betrayal, not just of my own good faith but of all that is comic. I didn't know that while I was watching him he was unconscious, which may have been a cock-eyed blessing, since he wouldn't remember the humiliation or the pain of falling out of time. In his sense of things, he wasn't even there.

NOT EXACTLY A SELF-INTERVIEW

Three postcards.

A 1961 cover of a paperback pulp novel, *Pushover* (by "Orrie Hitt"): "Gloria—Madeline—Sandy! EACH WAS EASY PICKIN'S." A redhead in a negligee stretches up from bed to kiss the man in a green suit looming over her. A keyhole frames the scene.

St. George Killing the Dragon, by one of my favorite painters, the short-lived (1331–69) Vitale da Bologna. St. George in a carmine tunic, blond locks flaming from his blue helmet, pitches forward, unsaddled, his lance staking the monster's head to the ground. Horse, man, and dragon are one knot of terror and contestation, as if each needs the other to fulfill its purpose in the world. And yet the picture's twisty turbulence resolves into an uncanny stillness.

An ancient relief of a bacchante, one of Dionysos's tripped-out followers. Her head droops, her knees buckle, her entire body weakens because it's filled with the god: physical erectness and self-possession loosen into rapture, dissolution, unreason. The god's power to disintegrate us shivers through the stone.

To these images that I've had over my desk for years I've added a newspaper photo taken after the 2001 Seattle quake. A firefighter in his bulging gear supports the arm of a woman wearing a fur-collar topcoat, sweater, and kid gloves. She looks down but not *at* anything, arms raised as if to ward off the helper. He's entirely in the moment, she's somewhere else. In time maybe I'll know why this image is compelling enough to take its place next to those others, which pinch my life a little every day.

When I write, especially if the work goes slowly, as it usually does, I tell myself that in time, if I'm prepared to receive, I'll know what a poem is offering me. A poem-in-process has an imagination of its own, a mysterious acrobatics of association and accident. While I work at it, it works toward me. If I finish a poem, and if it's real, that double action fuses into one arc of speech. I like to think that my little wall-tacked icons protect me from writing in bad faith, though no mojo guarantees that. Each has something to do with Eros—the vague lymphic power that sexualizes the world—or with unreason, or impending chaos. *PUSHOVER:* THE TORRID TALE OF A TOWN MORE WICKED THAN PEYTON PLACE! Each shows wildness or uncertainty coming into a form, into the restive momentary stability that a poem is.

When an editor proposed to tape an interview with me in connection with a book I'd published (*Skirts and Slacks*), I thought back to something I wrote twenty-five years ago: "The interview has become the most proliferating literary form of our time. Poets don't write critical prose. Instead of writing they talk, and the talk is recorded, published, then cited as authority in creative writing classrooms. Talk is cheaper than ever. And the interview serves and perpetuates the organizations of power in our playback culture." What to say about youth's high-toned arrogance and resistance? I was, back then, like certain marine creatures, puffed up and poisonous, but I still do believe that most official Creative Writing discourse is just another form of cable TV news analysis and celebrity magazine copy. All systems are the same system. Anyway, when I have to explain something, I feel more at ease writing than talking: I need a lot of time to make mistakes, so an interview clearly wasn't the way to go.

So I considered doing a self-interview, which has elegant precedents—the Italian poet Eugenio Montale composed a deliciously evasive interview with himself—but I knew I wouldn't feel easy with the faked chamber theatricality of the form. I finally decided to try to write plainspoken bits about the book and how I work, which I offer here with misgivings. Self-exposure makes me queasy. Over the years I've written about my poetry mostly behind the blind of something else. Whenever I published an essay collection and the marketing staff asked what the book was about, I said it was about me. (They loved hearing that.) Criticism is a public meditation and a private conversation. I've written about Hart Crane, Coleridge, Pier Paolo Pasolini, Tom McGrath, Pound, Giacometti, Bonnard, Matisse, and others because their work stirred up questions relevant to the poetry I write and to the life of poetry generally.

My prose is grounded in assumptions foundational to the poetry. I think we should call things by their real names. I dislike and distrust anything that abstracts us from physical reality, whether it's inauthentic poetry, theory-heavy criticism, opportunistic social analysis, or greased political promises. Like many poets, I can't talk about myself without talking about the echoing tonalities and sometimes unidentifiable voicings of previous poets. I try to recall things to keep me honest, like Browning's "The world's no blot for us nor blank. / It means intensely and means good. / To find its meaning is my meat and drink." Or to remind me of the task, the Wallace Stevens lines I've quoted elsewhere: "The poem is the cry of its occasion, / Part of the res itself and not about it. / The poet speaks the poem as it is, // Not as it was: part of the reverberation / Of a windy night as it is."

It's impossible not to seem coy or shameless saying this, but here it is: while going through my mother's closet after her death a few years ago, in a cigar box behind the rack of skirts and slacks, I found loaded and cocked the gun she and my father kept hidden for years, the one I played with as a kid rooting in secret places, sometimes sticking the barrel in my mouth. Finding it again rushed me back to the angers, silences, and humiliations of that house. The title of a poem occasioned by that experience, "Skirts and Slacks," seemed related by instinct (not deliberation) to poems I'd been writing about other deaths and dissolutions going on around me—poems I meant not to be about anecdotes but a reenactment of funerary rites—and about the fraying social order I saw when I walked the streets. My books start out as miscellanies. I don't go looking for subject matter and don't have "projects." I write out of compulsions, seizures, preoccupations. Born into the working-class, I probably had genetically encoded in me a sense of writing as a brick-by-brick, poem-by-poem process. If I work hard, if I'm lucky, the poems will disclose their themes.

So far as one can control such things, in an art punched forward by inchoate urgencies and instincts, I wanted that particular book, *Skirts and Slacks,* to enact truths of feeling about dying, sexual love, personal and public saneness. When I was small, adults criticized me for being too serious. (It wasn't seriousness, it was an almost pathological shyness.) When readers say my work generally is "serious," I cringe to think they mean somber, thick-browed. Poets have a deep, irrational sense of the rhythmic shape they want a poem to be. Mine involves mixed tones, jumpy cadences, sound-speeds. I'm not a comic poet (yet) or poet of joy (yet). The work issues from my feeling that the more we come into consciousness, the more we come into awareness of mortality, and that this isn't a melancholy or depressing recognition but a thrilling one because it completes us as humans. That there are no easy answers to anything, that sorrow is a complicated thing that may be simply put, that bittersweetness isn't something arrived at but a place to start—these persuasions run, by my lights, through most of what I've done the past fifteen years.

If poems come out right, they tell what it feels like to live in a world of troubled relatedness. They have to do with hungers and wants more than with satisfactions and consolations. I'm not interested in prettiness, correctness, formal high jinks, or local color. Poetry expresses temperament. Mine, to use the medieval formula, is melancholic-choleric, so any act of recollection is a fired-up desire to grasp something, or a vague realization of a task left unfinished. (Vagueness is essential to the work of poetry.) Drivenness, intensity, density, qualities I'm too familiar with, can make the work a prisoner to their moods. While writing *Skirts and Slacks* I was trying to work away from the chunky toiling and occasional dreaminess of earlier poems, away from their preoccupation with otherworldliness (though this will probably always haunt what I do) and toward a poetry more fastened to the physical world. I wanted something that would allow more rattle or wobble, a finer layering of feeling, a looser way of handling the paint.

Cities are what I know and love. I'm at ease in the different energy fields they create, and many of the poems in my books migrate, like me, from one cityscape to another (South Philly neighborhoods; the New York Port Authority; Haight Street; Boston's South End; Venice; Bologna), where actions occur in distressed interiors (saloon, cellar, hospital room, airplane, kitchen, church, train). Place isn't a housing for subject matter; it's the shape of experience. Place *is* memory, and remembering is an act of desire. By nature I'm a watcher or witness. From when I was a kid, I've given myself headaches by staring too hard at things. Reality appears first as an undifferentiated field, but in time hot particulars separate out and make claims on my consciousness. I don't so much choose subjects as they choose or—it can feel like wooing—come on to me. Characters in the poems are often modeled on real people—street people, family, lovers, friends. But the modeling process alters reality. (Baudelaire said that a portrait is a model complicated by the artist.) The imagination isn't a faculty but an act of pursuit, the chase to find something I didn't know I was looking for.

One day a friend was checking out those postcards above my desk. I was remembering that Carpaccio's St. George picture turned up in a poem I wrote years ago: a deranged woman babbles about her botched opportunity to assassinate Hitler when he visited Rome—she could have delivered civilization from barbarism. My friend was more interested in the *Pushover* image and its keyhole view. I told him I hadn't figured out why I found it compelling. He said: "It's because you've written that poem."

He was thinking of a thing in an earlier book occasioned by my entering, late one night in a foreign city, the wrong hotel room. The epigraph is from *Madame Bovary:*

The Hotel Room Mirror

But who was it, then, that made her so unhappy?
—Madame Bovary

A half-room, foreshortened even more
in the huge speckled armoire glass,
the distance chopped, uncrossable,
between your image and where I stood

twiddling the doorknob before I knew
my own key didn't fit, late night,
your interior so underlit
that bluer shadows oozed your forms.

Already too late, the door
breezed open where your back and thighs
twisted in the green-winged chair,
your body's light coiled, at rest.

Dressed, angled deeper in the surface,
your man pleaded, hands wide, as he flexed
sharp from the bed's protesting edge,
the sheets pin-wheeled beneath his weight.

Your glance and his (haphazard,
stark and unconcerned) found mine
in the frame, waiting, though I stayed
invisible to myself, my stare

like your bold forms inhabiting
our depth of field, in the scuffed glass
transcribed. It was already still
too late to save you or be saved.

A scene witnessed through a keyhole. The poem is a belated message to that woman, a feckless confession of failure to deliver her from some (completely imagined) erotic distress. It's also a message to myself and anybody who cares to listen. I don't mean to be contrary by speaking of a recent book by quoting from an old one. As I said, it's hard not to seem coy or full of myself. My point, really, is that I feel the world as a place where everything pressures or webs itself to everything else, and what I write expresses that feeling.

LATE ARRIVALS

Life stumbles over its own fact, for its earlier
moments plunge ceaselessly into later ones which
reinterpret and correct them.
—WILLIAM JAMES

I

Like most writers, when I'm working well, I'm in a fugue state, unaware of remembering or forgetting. In a fugue state, neuroscience tells us, one is unaware of having lost all sense of personal identity. It's also physically dissociating, dreamily so—chronic pain I've lived with for forty years subsides, as it does in beatific dreams—and I'm living in lost time, in oblivion induced by the process of work. It's a form of inspiration, an auto-hypnosis instrumented by Muse or God or neural network. (It's not peculiar to writers and artists: mathematicians, systems analysts, and cabinetmakers experience the same state.) I get lost in the now but lost to something past, since writing is practically all recovery. I look down at whatever's under my nose, then look up and it's three or four hours later. Where have I been? In what labyrinth?

Other times I feel the utterness of the instant, its pastlessness. In a New England wood, away from traffic noise, I lie on the ground or sit on a rock. The wind blows hard; the birches, maples, and poplars rattle; leaves zip through the air, changing speed and direction with menacing quickness. In the moment, only these sensations exist. They mark the limits of consciousness and seal me in what I imagine to be the present, because they don't deliver me to any past event. But I also know it's not an eternal present, a fiction we can imagine but never experience, because there is no moment, really. The apparition of the instant is smashed by what fills it—leaves, wind, trees, a broil of pure becoming.

Another kind of oblivion, a different storminess, comes over me at my neighborhood streetcar stop in the early A.M., an ecstasy, like my moment in the woods, but induced by bodies and city engines, most of all by scents scrambled around and through the crowd. Who's wearing Chanel? What shampoo was that? Who's gusting that warm-milk-and-coffee breath with hints of sugar donut? And somebody must have had licorice for breakfast. It's not at all like being in the woods, because every piece—smells are like substances, with shapes, textures, weights—hinges to another experience, another story, a memory network that's already making rapid-fire connections while I'm recalling what seems to be the first of such connections. But I don't experience a sequence of any kind, let alone organized. I experience only the tremendous pressure of liquid relatedness impacted, calcified, in an instant—one gulp—of time.

✡

Now in my early sixties, I perversely want more and more what I know to be impossible: to write a poetry erased of memory that expresses only the experienced instant, a pattern of words that's just a grain of sand dropped in the eye. I'm reminded of Courbet's remark in a letter to Proudhon: "The past is useful only as education. One must use only the present in one's work. Banish the mysterious, the miraculous, don't believe in the incomprehensible." Memory: mysterious, miraculous, incomprehensible. Except that neuroscience each day comes closer to demystifying memory and describing an even greater mystery-generating grandeur living in the physiological complexities of its origins and functions. Imagine galaxy clusters as fine needlework. I've made so much for so long, to myself and to anyone who would listen, about memory's importance—Homer tells how Apollo stripped memory from the poet who dared to challenge the Muses—I get sick with it. When recollection drives or takes over a poem, the poem becomes nauseated by it. I tell myself I want pure breakneck invention, as if invention could be separated from recollection. Partly this comes from the middle-aged fear of waking to find I've already lived a life but haven't quite lived it out. I'm temperamentally constructed so that it would be easy to slouch into memory and lose the nervous momentum poetry feeds on, the tumbling into and through circumstance. "The way through the world," Stevens says in one of his poems, "is more difficult to find than the way beyond it." The Sirens' harp and kazoo noise lures us to the always-blooming sea garden of the past, which we value because it's *ours*, but with that comes the cheap allure of local color, exoticism, special pleading, and bittersweet preciosity which, however true to life, have no place in real poetry. So I tell myself to put my head down and keep walking into the wind, guided by William James's pragmatic notion that thoughts are instrumental, "mental modes of adaptation to reality, rather than revelations or gnostic answers to some divinely intuited world-enigma." Everything connects or relates to something else, but nothing includes or dominates everything. "The word 'and,'" James says, "trails along after every sentence."

Except for poetry grounded in Buddhist belief, instantaneity of feeling, thought, and word is an illusion, albeit a sustaining one. No such moment exists, not for a Western sensibility like mine anyway, though I can imagine its existence and even pretend that I live in a pristine moment that burns in and around me, its cool fire aloof from moments that precede or follow it. But then I catch myself and think that whatever's consequential turns on time's wheel and is an act of recovery or recollection or restoration. So much is bound up in this—personal and public experience and histories and all the finely layered imagined or reinvented tissues of experience. Well, buster, throw that dust to the wind. Awareness thus purged, I'll be able to make a poetry free of memory's climates and debris, its hecatombs, bubblegum wrappers, ditties, and was that really Chanel or was it Safeway shampoo? No possibility excites me more. To live and write out of a constantly self-renewing present. Except that cognitive science tells us that such a slot in time, while we can imagine it, doesn't exist. The neuroscientist Antonio Damasio, who gives such accurate reports of how we feel time, says: "Present continuously becomes past, and by the time we take stock of it we are in another present, consumed with planning the future, which we do on the stepping stones of the past. The present is never here. We are hopelessly late for consciousness."

2

Many years ago, working at my desk, living with what I didn't then know were daily erosions that would result in a broken marriage and broken self,

I experienced a click in consciousness, a broken circuit, on-off-on, and for an instant the ordinary involuntary momentum of sensation and thought ceased, then just as quickly reignited, as if I'd lapsed into some sort of unconsciousness while still conscious. The involuntary ongoing sensation of being in a real world stopped. I was, for however long the spell lasted, dropped from time. It terrified me because it was a little total abyss of oblivion in the normal stream of the everyday, some mysterious neural event in which millions of nerve cells, or so it felt, stopped firing.

I had a similar experience later, with a difference. Nothing tore, but I felt I'd dropped from my moment into all time, into a disorienting, undifferentiated, but unified smear in consciousness, incited by (no surprise here) a taste, which warped me into another dimension, an experience different from Proust's spoonful of tea and madeleine crumbs, because it didn't instrument a reinvention of lost time. It wasn't at all like the "exquisite pleasure" young Marcel took from that taste, which recalled his privileged days at Combray, a surging joy that erased his feeling of being "mediocre, contingent, mortal." Mine did the opposite: it made me feel even more vulnerable and mortal, it didn't release a mysterious, all-powerful happiness, it shook me up, because I was certain I was sounding something foundational but unknowable. I'm not sure I even wanted to know what was waiting to be found. It was at any rate an inauspicious occasion: I tasted soy milk for the first time. Vanilla flavored. It had the kind of profound baffling familiarity that jellies your viscera, but it didn't connect me to an originating event, which was long gone, I thought, so I was lost to something I'd never identify. What primed me for that? I thought it might be my old familiar, Signor Coyote, prankster imagination, drawing me into a half-lit room only to juke and mock me.

✡

Mnemosyne. Mother of the Muses. It was Mama all along, calling for me, it turned out, though *la mamma vera* was long dead, and not really Mama anyway but her milk, or rather *not* her milk because she, my actual mother, didn't breast-feed me. I was, like so many in my postwar generation, a bottle baby—it makes us sound like lab animals—and the key ingredient in formula was soy. Samuel Beckett liked to say he could remember being in his mother's womb. I think we probably all do but lack proper instruments, or Beckett's preternatural intuition, to access the sensation. (If we could, we might hate being alive and commit mass suicide.) My middle-aged taste of soy delivered me back to that sucking, slurping, burping hunger that feels preconscious, it was recollection burned into tongue and throat. From that experiential moment I brought nothing back, except the recognition. I knew little more about myself or reality than I had a minute before. But I was changed, psychically roughed-up. I'd inhaled something so deep in my being that it identified *me* as *it*, and *it* as *me*, and my passion in that instant was to recover the source. Not to do so would be to increase the ways in which I remain unknown to myself, ogling unidentifiable bits of rag and flesh and dirt and wings in Mother's silken sticky web.

We think we experience a memory as a photographic instant or cine-matic sequence, but that's an illusion. The brain crafts remembrance as a composite of information networked from different regions of the cortex. Some researchers say we don't remember events, we remember remembering. The brain recovers and recalls not experience but its own reconstruction of it over time. We think it's always the same Aunt Maggie we're remem-bering, Damasio says, but she's a different Aunt Maggie every time. Words themselves are such memory bearers, not only in their meanings but in their physical attributes—sound, texture, speed—that a lyric poem is hopelessly an enactment and analogue of memory. It remembers remembering, craves whatever's foundational, and moves two ways at once: it wants to articulate the tremulousness and solidity and haunted viscosities of actual experience while drilling through the strata of experience to some bedrock, whatever it may be. Memory is anxiety. My psychic event, that click, occurred while I was trying to write a poem that caught up the disordered states—personal, domestic, communal—I was then living through. It wanted to predict the present. My brain may have shut down to avoid or defer that.

3

I'm recalling a fall morning in 2003 spent reading and thinking about recol-lection and memory models. Later that morning I go to the farmer's market and at a bakery stand buy a roll which, when I tear off a piece, has the hollow center and hard crust of a bread I ate a hundred times when I lived in Italy.

I can't remember what it's called, so I'm on a mission, a market mission. I'm looking for something I'm not sure waits to be found. What's it called? The question even comes to mind in Italian. *Questo pane come si chiama?* Perfectly round, chewy, lightly salted, and delectable.

An engram—the term coined by Richard Semon, a nineteenth-century German biologist who studied the way neural networks preserve experience over time—is essentially the representation of a memory in the brain. I learn this, while getting coffee before market, from Daniel Schacter's *Searching for Memory: The Brain, The Mind, and The Past*. Engrams, he says, "are the transient or enduring changes in our brains that result from encoding an experience." Different parts of the brain are engaged in the encoding of experience, and every encoding therefore strengthens the connections, the fields of relatedness, between different neural networks performing different tasks. "The new pattern of connections constitutes the brain's record of the event: the engram." When we use mental tricks or memory models to access past events, we're looking for ways to cue the engram. Sometimes we cue it by recalling the environment in which a memory occurred (source memory). The lack of any one or combination of these capabilities results in the many pathologies of remembrance.

✡

So, that roll. *Come si chiama?* Nothing wrong with my source memory. I can practically taste the engram—creamy unsalted butter, autumns in Bologna, smells of coffee and roasting chestnuts blowing through the streets. Today's list: bread, eggs, heirlooms, and apples. Nothing wrong with what Schacter calls "episodic" memory, the recollection of a specific event or anecdote. What I fail to get is the harmonic, the set of sounds that effectively constitute the thing in my consciousness. I need help, so I go back to the baker, but she calls it by some dialect word I've never heard.

Whenever I have a strong source memory but can't remember the name of the thing in the episode, I run an exercise that combines visualization and vocalization. I start at "A" and work through the alphabet, at each letter playing sound variants—vowels, then diphthongs and consonants—off the initial, which triggers or casts a shapely shadow of the completed word. B-a ...baratry. B-oi...boilersuit. B-ra...bratwurst. The system favors vowel-rich Italian. So I start at "A" and get all the way to "P" and "S," skipping "Q" because I know that can't be right (Italian has very few "Q" words), but by that point I'm hurrying and realize I jumped sequence and forgot to test "R." As soon as I have that thought, that awareness of something I forgot, the word bumps my brain. *Rosetta.* I find it without initial cueing. It rises like a pure lyric, pressured into form by context and routine, waiting to be found but until then nonexistent except as desire or foreshadowing or intuition. Mechanically mysterious. Give me the past anytime. But *give* it.

4

Some poets believe Mother Memory isn't relevant. A contemporary, responding to something I'd said in an interview, once remarked that I was some kind of Wordsworthian mooncalf, that poets who think as I do are writing out of an obsolescent Romantic presupposition, that one shouldn't make such a fuss about poetry as recovered subjectivity. He had a point. Recollection of personal experience can't be the only motor that powers the imagination; pragmatic invention is just as important. And yet to dish memory's elaborations, falsifications, and crackpot inventiveness, along with the world of subjectivity it so critically shapes (and which shapes *it*), is to give up radical curiosity about what we are, chemically as well as spiritually. Or spiritual *because* chemical. In the past fifty years, brain researchers have practically created an alternate universe seemingly as expansive and finely articulated as our own, except that it really is our own, and it's not only in our heads. We are what we network, or what our bundles of nerve cells and their extensive axions that shoot and hook them to other cellular networks make us. It's where deity lives. Something as trivial as my *rosetta* expedition (which would have been cued immediately if I'd been *looking*—the crust bears a roseate design) keeps me alert, because recollection in poetry (or art of other kinds) is more than mere occasion, it's a plasmic shape-shifting energy. Nietzsche wasn't being fanciful when he said he thought and wrote with his entire body. Neurocircuitry is so densely webbed, the brain is so much the organic locale of thought and sensation, that the body thinks, the mind feels.

When I see models or resonance imagings of the brain, I visualize sensory information of the past—species past and individual past—tucked like minute flakes and dust particles within its convolutions, immateriality enfolded by spongy matter, the hiding places of our power. That's where writers go for memory traces, the engrams hidden or dropped by time into those folds, which look like fissures, openings that conceal. The going is usually driven by associative sensation, which recalls to life some reinvention, reconstruction, or reimagination of something we think once was. These recognitions then get brought over into particular words in a particular order. The pursuit isn't for the *rosetta* itself so much as for the episode, the chain of experiences, encoded in the emblem. Recollection compounds originating event and times between, between it and me, then and now.

5

I had no poetry mentors in college and was intellectually formless. I took instruction from whichever poets came my way, with little more than chronology, crude taste, and instinct to lead me. Visual artists became exemplars, too, and I wanted to emulate them, since every art—music, dance, writing—seemed to converse with some other and all were in the business of form-finding. I don't mean to dignify this. I was raw, green, mule-headed, and fearful of being found out: I was hideously unprepared for serious study and as hideously primitive in using words. But I was dog-face serious and must have cut an amusing figure. I read poets, like Whitman and Crane, who excited me, and I was incoherently enthusiastic about the life of poetry in history and as a possible life for myself. Close by was the Philadelphia Museum of Art, which was foundational in two ways: I got the rudiments of art history there, and it had significant holdings of artists who became big in my life, especially Paul Klee and Alberto Giacometti. They taught me more about being a poet than the poets I was reading, who taught me sounds and rhythms. I've revisited Giacometti's work many times since, but to judge by a recent experience, Klee has all along been a more insinuating presence. When I first saw his 1938 *Fish Magic* (it's in Philadelphia's permanent collection) it literally pushed me back. Its mysteriousness—fishy and floral shapes and cages and nets fused to what looks like watery air—somehow intensified and destabilized reality and me. I saw it again in a retrospective nearly thirty-five years ago, along with paintings and graphics from Klee's entire career. Nearly every picture was a hermetic culture of unexpectedness in which familiar objects were turned into suggestive, enigmatic, bitingly beautiful forms. The image inventiveness got under my skin and stayed there. The wirework and webbing woven or built into human figures (and animals and plants) became the objects they contained. A man in a cage was a cage composed of a man. Such inquiring art is made at the nerve ends, which we can now fairly say is art made in (and made up of) the mind. Klee's vision was aboriginal, like the vision of the poets I was drawn to. The more an artist looks at the finished forms of nature, he said, "the more readily he can extend his view from the present to the past, the more deeply he is impressed by the one essential image of creation itself, as Genesis, rather than by the image of nature, the finished product."

Recently, after years of pretty much ignoring his work, I saw a smallish Klee show in San Francisco that rattled me top to bottom, inside and out, not because the pictures were choice or recalled my initiation experience in Philadelphia but because they were a blunt unitary hit of whole-body remembrance. They tripped the memory of a life—its ambition, disorder, ignorance—lived many years ago. Klee's *Absorption,* a comic drawing (and self-portrait), shows a square, squinty face in a state of absurdly intense concentration, maniacally serious, which I joltingly remembered myself to have been, though I certainly didn't know it at the time. The drawing was in and about *my* time. It seemed to be remembering itself in my moment. Most of the pictures in the show didn't just recall that gestalt, they constituted it. Losing myself to an oceanic sustained moment occasioned by a picture, I was just as much in any other discrete moment that intervened between then and now. I was delivered to myself as a young vague thing with an ambition to be a poet, who believed in pure lyric, which *Fish Magic* is.

The forms helped induce that swoon. Klee's line is exploratory, anxious; his colors scrim and veil the very ground they compose. He liked to say that the artist makes the invisible visible. His imagery often expresses awestruck skepticism, or skeptical awe, in the presence of a vaguely spiritualized material world. His drawing can be so scant and ephemeral that it's like a not quite recovered memory—from twelve feet away marks become a faint drizzle in consciousness, the geometries and volumes so evanescent that recognizable figures come into shape and undo themselves as one pictorial action. My whole-body remembrance made me think that when I'm writing I'm somehow remembering these old sources, even if I'm unaware. I'm under water and don't know I'm drowning.

6

Lost time isn't always time lost. Most of my adult life I've wanted to learn to live in the moment, not to migrate so instinctually to past events or flash forward to circumstances that don't even yet exist, but it now seems to me that much of life gets lived, and much writing written, in unforeseeable ruptures, descents, and absentings, that when we truly live in the moment, we live in an off-ness, a condition we hardly recall the contents of, though we're certain of its occurrence. If true, it helps explain why we're the happiest and sorriest of creatures. Poetry is the deposit of such experience.

Writing this, I've sometimes felt grafted onto the tissue of the words themselves, stuck in some weird membranous mass, like a Klee invention. I kept losing my way and sense of self, all the while hoping to escape an impasse in my work and break through to I know not what, maybe to write truly off my nerves, but coherently, so that a feeling for the world of facts will be loaded into every phrase and words will be—as I crudely imagined they could be when I was young—both greeting and enactment. I'd like a poetry that restores the knowledge, felt knowledge, that we're always late arriving but doing all we humanly can, hopelessly trying to be on time for consciousness.

The challenge to this comes, as I should have foreseen, from William James, whose investigations of consciousness were always strummed by the nearness of derangement. "The moment stands and contains and sums up all things," he says, "and all change is within it, much as the developing land-scape with all its growth falls forever within the rear windowpane of the last car of a train that is speeding on its headlong way. This self-sustaining in the midst of self-removal, which characterizes all reality and fact, is absolutely foreign to the nature of language." But language, I think, can act out the sensation of the moment in its fugitive changes. A fact-bound, fact-hounded poet like myself needs to be reminded that fact can be vaporous nuance, even or especially the re-confabulated facts of memory, and that the language of poetry, as hard and solid as one can make it, pursues that spirit essence.

INSIDE THE BOX

I hear him without seeing him, the pallid, knobby, slightly seedy gentleman in jazz-bow who sets up his electronic keyboard in neighborhoods around San Francisco. Sometimes he's on the corner where I catch the streetcar I'm now riding—a thundering gun-gray ironclad made in Italy—plinking "Kitten on the Keys" or "Lucy in the Sky with Diamonds," though at the moment I've just exited the tunnel that runs under Yerba Buena Park, a great green mound in the Haight created by centuries of sand blown from the ocean two miles west. The tunnel's east portal opens onto Duboce Park where, because I'm watching nannies huddle with toddlers in the playlot and dogs chase lofty round objects across the lawn, I miss seeing him but moments later catch the back draft of a nasal "Ode to Joy." The musician is Joseph Cornell.

In Milan's Piazza del Duomo one Sunday afternoon—it's Y2K now—where the great grotesque white basilica looms like a gargoyle watching us all, tourists meander and gather amongst well-heeled Milanese at their *passeggiata,* cool teens making out or goofing to boom box rap, Serbs and Albanians in bright rayon running suits, Africans hawking knockoff watches, handbags, scarves. Beyond the square, beyond the file of trams outside the colonnade, the hotel where I usually stay waits again for me on Via Speronari, an alleyway really, *un vicolo,* strangely tranquil for being so close to the Duomo, though what I'm remembering, riding my N-Judah car, here and now in 2007, isn't a particular lobby with a particular desk but a feeling tone, the pleasurable off-ness of a foreign place—threadbare faux-Persian runner; warmly dim corridors poor of wattage; filmy curtains dripping from Baroque finials and wrought iron rings; bovine armoire partly lined with yellowing Italian newsprint. Once I've checked in and feel flush with that familiar alienated completeness of being in a foreign place, I look outside the window and hear trams around the corner, out of sight, grinding off toward La Scala and satellite piazzas. I feel at ease but estranged, as if in a place I've often visited but never really been *inside* till now, as one never forgets the feeling of being *inside* a cave or ship's cabin or shut closet. I'm in Joseph's Cornell's basement.

I switch transport and now ride in a Milan tram down Market Street in San Francisco, the same train—recollection's mirrored chambers suggest to me—I rode when I lived in Italy in the early 1970s, or that other one I rode near Via Speronari in 2000. Same tawny tangerine exterior piped with rivets; cartouche body; wooden benches running on both sides of a broad aisle; molar-crunching steel wheels. The original signage exhorts me to buy a certain olive oil, *100% Puro Naturale,* but there must be invisible wires of consciousness in the air, or neurological fractals popping and trumpeting one to another, because I feel delivered back to Philadelphia in the 1950s, heaven help me, riding the Tenth Street trolley, forehead pressed to the glass, eyeballing the huge shadow boxes of Gimbel's window displays, jeweler's row, hoagie pits, Dickensian apothecaries, five-and-dimes, and candy stores marked with big tin badges die-stamped FRANK'S BLACK CHERRY WISHNIAK. How lovely it is, so unlike the dandified Milan casket, this Pullman Philadelphia Transit Company trolley, a green steel-wheels helmet, stubby wings swept behind the PTC logo, and inside it, furtive me. The squeal and rumble, the vibrations tickling the vinyl seats, the streaming scenes outside—it feels natural, this fibrillated ongoingness of isolated bits of the real and the obsessively remembered, of a squinty playfulness fraught with something ineffable, a stirring in the cosmos of consciousness momentarily stilled, like the contents of a Cornell shadow-box. Several years ago San Francisco created the "F" line of renovated vintage trolleys from Milan, Philadelphia, Chicago, and assorted elsewheres, which run the eastern length of town from the Castro to the Embarcadero, restored remnants of a past that *must* have been an improvement on our present: even if we never experienced that past, we can and want to imagine we did, so we do. They're hermetic zones of migrant sensations, of regret, elation, curiosity, where each discrete thing exists in precise relation to some other: taken together—wraith-ish, achingly presumptuous, and suggestive—they don't narrate, they haunt. Mallarmé said he wanted to make poetry that was all "evocation, allusion, suggestion," one that possessed a "universal musicality." A doll in one Cornell box stands (hangs? levitates?) in a twiggy, stripped-bare wood.

So I'm riding Chicago's "L" south one early evening toward the Loop and my train pulls into the Howard Street switching station, where lines converge from shuntings and two northbound routes. This 2004 night I see—it lasts maybe five seconds—two trains in the middle distance running at different elevations on separate but parallel tracks, so that one appears to roll piggyback on the other, just as Milan trams and PTC trolleys run in my head. Bells, horns, sirens. Nocturnes. Romance and danger. It's late, in South Philly circa 1962, where I've been visiting a prospective girlfriend, what Joseph Cornell called, when speaking of young girls he had crushes-without-consequence on, a "teener," and I walk in on a trolley car robbery, the conductor pinned to the floor by two guys, one with a gun, who turns and jabs it at me. I jump off and run. He gives chase and is fleet of foot, goddamn it, waving that *pistola,* but I know the alleys and he doesn't. A summer night. I remember the visibility of stars I certainly wasn't then cognizant of, the sensation of running, I'm recalling only now writing this, housing the sensation here in this safe deposit box. The stretched, spasmic episode is shrink-wrapped into one moody, daffy-associative, daintily articulated moment. And anytime I remember it, neuroscience instructs me, it's a different moment made of diverse info accessed from parts of the brain to construct what I "see" as the same event. It's a revised story whose seams don't show. Cornell always built the boxes first, and then revised by putting things in or taking them out. His Aviary, Hotel, Penny Arcade, and Medici children series, each box in a series different from another, all look alike. See one for the first time and you're convinced you've seen it before.

It happens in intenser moments, though the casual has its own intensities. Things present and past start answering to each other, pulsing signals back and forth. Each thing is quite clear and identifiable—gun, fretted basilica marble, hardwood benches, cappacolla and prosciutto, sapphires, black cherry wishniak. They could be soap-bubble pipes, clock springs, European signage, Frenchie cockatoos, newspapers, latticed thimble-size mirrors, velvet-lined jewel cases. Their being in relation to each other makes sense, but the entire scene does not. It's nothing like a dream state where things have a lurid specificity as part of a liquid, lava-lamp narrative. It's an intensification of the real and of our experience of it. It sharpens perception and appetite the way sexual desire does, though the artist Cornell—who couldn't draw and lived into his sixties mostly in a house on Utopia Parkway in Flushing, Queens, with his sweet-natured, severely palsied brother (who drew better than Joseph) and their asphyxiating mother—never had sex. Dreams get fixed in the amber of their own queer, jangled logic. Cornell's boxes' contents are tranquilized but conductive. If the world really is Baudelaire's forest of symbols in which scents, sounds, and textures blend one with another, each with every other, and if artists live in a wakeful process somehow in a constant seizure state of cosmic analogies, we have to stay them, give them some temporary ordering, as a holding action, to keep from drowning in the pleasurable idiocy of shapeless sensation.

Soap bubbles drift this way and that. In Duboce Park, young girls skip rope. Cornell was distressed when the Third Avenue El was demolished in 1955 and a year later writes in his journal of a visionary El moment: "rose-orange near building lavender—grey haze over Manhattan skyline—across the freight yards in twilight and across the river the El curving round almost full sweep circle in Queens Plaza—reminder of profound sense again of this benedictory beauty 'the American scene.'" We look into a box and a foreign newspaper or menu or timetable lining a wall, only partly legible, may be more or less so next time we visit. The stars shine from their blue background of paper astrology charts. Still stars. The boxes don't move but feel aquiver with memory's complex, elusive nonce immediacy. What's to be said when ping-pong balls make a music of the spheres that the imagination conjures but can't be heard by human ears? Strangest when most familiar, some mechanism, neural, phantasmal, sets the image-patterns at a remove, like strangers who remind us of those we know and love. Cornell admired Mallarmé, and the hints of unconscious or preconscious states of mind evoked in Mallarmé's poems inspired him to synthesize imagery and materials from wildly diverse sources, much as the brain accesses and networks all sorts of debris to assemble memories. Cornell's mysterious hermetic rooms, sites of what

Breton called "the marvelous," don't try to pattern information and sensation into organized units answerable to reason; they express the condition of being memory-haunted, of an intense but slightly giddy excitability of living in a moment we know we can never really know. We're always at the threshold of a world not yet formed, though everything necessary seems to be already there. A darkened 12" × 8" box on a wall conceals a flat curved shape: press the illumination button and the shape jumps out as an owl, foregrounded on a leafy backdrop, backlit by that bluish hue. *Scarlatti's Owl*. Meaning what, exactly? Nothing, exactly, because it has no statement content. Cornell is all articulated traceries of what can't be said. His owl bears toward us—the glass cover turns content into specimens in a vitrine, observable but remote—menacing suspicion, watchful, a little censorious but formal, courtly.

Mallarmé's poems dissolve into a sacral sensibility scrutinizing its own movements. It's a priestly effort, but poems, even his, are secular facts: Mallarmé's church was built of words. Joseph read and loved Mallarmé's work but formed the self-revising perceptions into a magically evocative specificity of *items*. Mallarmé's impressions respire and expire one into another, his items shift from state to state, from solid to vapor to liquid, but Cornell's objects can't help but possess a Yankee fixity. They *encounter* each other—that's the feeling for this observer—or happen to be fated to exist in a certain deoxygenated relation to something else in their showcase environs. Cornell loved Houdini's tricks, and the boxes are now-you-see-them-(me)-now-you-don't stage acts. His journals, like the boxes, have an animal immediacy and oneiric elusiveness. (A pink, sparkle-dusted chateau with tiny mirror windows is encroached on by a twiggy choked copse, the same wherein elsewhere hangs the baby doll.) They, the journals, record how we begin to lose something the moment vision colonizes it. Feelings attached to memories flare and fade, and the more things pile up the greater the sensation of loss and yearning. An entry dated "Feb. 24, 1956 5 P.M." begins with a bus ride, snack ("Bickford nice doughnut and drink"), and the acquisition of a Mahler symphony and green stationery.

> 6:25 en route El subway <u>snow!</u> Skyline dirty haze—mean cold-found
> "Lélia"—neck pressure—borderline mood—nervousness but not on
> verge of uncontrollable—last eve—saw teenager for 1st time in year—
> seems completely changed—even physically—hardly recognized

her—had been library many times without seeing her (Barbara)—
memories of Xmas package for her year ago left anon—period of
"Scarlatti Parrot" (Xmas 1955)—things like this of which one might
expect such an opportunity to do more than just a diary note—come
and go too easily (from former changed state of mind)

Nothing *seems* fixed in his boxes, though every element is. Each wooden
ball seems about to roll. Birds give no sign of recent alighting or imminent flight. Feathers all over the place. A swan in a box (cut-out lakeside
backdrop) fixed inside a box loosely packed with feathers. Inside another,
a feather and faceless pocket-watch: tucked in an upper corner, like a celestial object, a folded typescript of a Mallarmé sonnet, who made a poetry
of shape-shifting marvels in which just as an image is coming into shape
it bleeds into yet another that comes and goes like smoke or starlight, with
the delayed illumination of starlight, like the effect of many of J.C.'s boxes,
so mysteriously designed to keep us out that they of course draw us in,
turning us into kids who, as mystical Yeats said of material Keats, rub their
noses on a candy store's window. Appetite and illusion, coming and going.
King Tantalus, punished by the gods for stealing their food and giving it to
mortals, is currently spending eternity in water up to his neck, a fruit-laden
tree above his head: when he leans to drink, the water evaporates; when he
stretches to taste the fruit, it blows away.

He never thought of the boxes as sculpture. They were settings for attain-
able unattainables, like a train running alongside the Interstate at night,
small movements astir behind the yellow-lighted glass. Dream images that
are versions of facts and that flirt with us when we're most susceptible.
Glamour girls, dusty starlets like Sheree North, undines, ballerinas, storybook children. The contents have a dummy specificity, terrifically isolate but
echolating, each object lassoing toward another a shadow meaning, a nuance,
a hint of magisterial consequence, always a whisper, not a shout. Each is a
storage unit of mysteries-as-pentimenti. Some dealers and collectors believe
Cornell boxes contain spirits. When one fell off a table and broke open, its
owners insisted that the piece had been destroyed, although the only object
that broke was a replaceable drinking glass. The owners protested that the
spirit had escaped the box and that the piece was therefore a total loss. The
insurers paid.

NOWHERE TO RUN

The top-down convertible slows, or seems to, as it passes. The woman inside, as I remember this, moves in slow motion, too. In her late twenties, early thirties maybe, though it's hard to tell, was hard to tell even then in the blurred action of car and face as they creamed into the night air, summertime, our car windows open, my father at the wheel, as background the dark green of a city park, a storybook forest that children vanish into. She was shouting "Help. Help me." A Shakespeare character would shout back: "What kind of help?" That's what I wanted to know, what kind. Though the man driving wasn't holding her, the terror and desperation sounded real, though she was also smiling, as if it were all a joke or ruse. They were pulling past and away from us, while I asked my father what was happening to her. "Nothing probably," he said. "How would I know?" I felt confused and sinful in my ignorance. Not taking action to save her *was* an act. But we invent or contrive possible actions in the wake of bad events. What could I have done? Or my father? I must have been ten or eleven years old. Those questions even then were tuning conscience to nerves. Some of memory's picture-strips stay more immediately available all one's life than others that may be even more momentous in consequence. This had to do vaguely—its vagueness is essential to its tenacity in memory—with panicked recognition of horror and danger attached to love, and love (or passion, anyway) attached to speed, hilarity, and ignorance.

■

For my family, New Year's Eve was always an event of strained celebration. People lived such aggrieved lives all year long that year's end was an occasion to let grievances go, for a while, and pretend noisily that promise and hope awaited. Our entire large family gathered at someone's house. Women got tipsy, which was unusual. Men had license to drink harder than usual. Husbands smoked Camels, their wives Pall Malls or Chesterfields. Everybody craved reassurance—who does not?—that they had reasons to be happy in their lives. I was young and wanted the New Year already to be over with. The ball over Times Square glittered on TV, and the adults watched in wonderment and anticipation as if not from Philadelphia but from India or Egypt. Were they celebrating the end of an old year or the beginning of a new one? Relief or foreboding? Nobody died this year, thank God. God is good even if he treats us bad, that God who, in Sinatra theology, was The Man Upstairs. Champagne, of course, the only time of year a beer-and-shot culture so indulged. Once, while people up and down the street stumbled outdoors, banging pots and pans, kissing neighbors, throwing fireworks (or not—my father nearly blew off his thumb lighting a firecracker in his hand), I tracked a scene: Bridget, a black-haired beauty who lived down the street, was running from her boyfriend (a tough, muscled Irishman), fear and rage in her face, while the boyfriend chased after, caught up, and grabbed her by the arm so hard she winced and started to cry. They struggled and were in each other's face so fiercely it looked as if all the celebratory energy of the night was suddenly channeled darkly between them. Everybody else is filled with the enthusiasm of the moment and doesn't see what's happening. The memory-strip runs out there, dissolves into whistles, smoke, hooting and horn-blowing.

Jump forward twelve years. I'm coming home after midnight, struggling to walk with canes because of a crippling ailment. Again, a woman goes past me, shouting, running, behind her a young guy who, like Bridget's boyfriend, finally grabs her. Then he slaps her. She groans and starts to run again. I give chase. That is, I mince pathetically behind, shouting at the guy to leave her alone, shouting so loudly that neighbors poke their heads from doors. This was an old-style, self-policing sort of neighborhood. Within seconds, it seemed, a half dozen men, some in pajamas, a few carrying baseball bats, are running down the guy to step between him and the girl, though the guy, temper aflame from the booze we all smell, is prepared to take it to the baseball bats, by which time a couple of squad cars pull up to settle the trouble. The pain that prevented me from moving and the immobility itself—like the sustained pause between times that is New Year's Eve—fuses to the running men, the girl, and her wolverine boyfriend.

Some years later the convertible girl in distress revisited me. This time I was on foot, walking by a city park, a sedan rolled past, windows open. A shrill cry, like wind gashing the air, warped through space and for that instant filled it. I couldn't tell if it was another call for help or a shout of gaiety. Just like the convertible girl. I wasn't alone. I was walking with a woman. We were in love and breaking up, croaking stupid words we hoped would never become too consequential, to fill time until we got to the train she would board that would take her far away. Erotic trauma so fills consciousness that the smallest details—leaf, gravel, dust—seem fraught, and we feel that the slightest twitch in the order of things will have shattering consequences. When I asked what to do about the wailing woman, she didn't understand. She didn't hear it, she said, she thought it was the wind. I was in so much chaos, had so much noise in my consciousness, that just then I began to doubt I'd even heard the voice at all.

✿

I remember some of the faces attached to these anecdotes, though they have a glassy visionary cast which, if I think too long, gets marbled by matter and its corruptions. Black-haired Bridget, my train station girl, where and how are they now? Puffy? Gaunt? Eyes pouchy, hair gray and thin, and teeth yellowed like mine? I've just gotten an e-mail—it's April 2005—from the woman I walked to the station twenty years ago, a sweet-tempered touch zizzing through fiber-optic networks that suddenly crosses with the memory of a late night in a bar, washed over by acidic reds and greens, when we'd drunk too much, shot pool, watched a fight break out where one guy kept trying to bite the other guy's ear, ate peanuts from the shell and (it was the bar's fame to encourage this) dumped the shells on the floor while Marvin Gaye wailed over our heads about sexual healing.

Because movies, even realistic ones, so seldom craft a recognizable shared reality, I was surprised a few years ago by a Hollywood product that treated the life of Aileen Wuornos, a truck-stop prostitute now on death row for killing several of her johns. I can't say how accurate the characterization was, but what the moviemakers get exactly right is her milieu: smoky honky-tonks, trailer parks, truckers' cafes, and hooker motels. It's the only world the Wuornos character knows how to inhabit—her interview for a straight, skirt-and-heels office job is catastrophic—because she more or less understands the rules, but the rules are really the misrule of instinct, unreason, and action without thought of consequence. Combine, with unquestioned regularity, heavy boozing, crummy job, sexual appetite, and the hope of not having to think about tomorrow (because it induces despair or revs up delusional hopes) and you end up with bar fights, quick rough-and-tumble sex, and drunken proclamations of keen ambitions and fresh starts—independence, travel, fat city. I knew a man (both in our early twenties then) clever but feckless and without prospects, who liked to drink. He conceived an ambition to make his way as a stand-up comedian, since he could, when sober, make people laugh. He'd hit the clubs and wait to be called to the stage but drank so hard and fast that when he finally made it to the mike, he was incoherent, so he tanked every time.

In those days, I was freeloading off a family kind enough to let me sleep on their sofa, where the would-be comic and his wife, one of three daughters in the house, also lived. I was tossing about in my own disorder. I'd lived in Philadelphia all my days and graduated from a local college where I lost a year because of a rheumatic illness that put me in the hospital for months, left me slow and gimpy (and unable to come to the aid of distressed damsels), and made my lower back a kiln that fired up when I slept on that lumpish sofa. I was there in the first place because my own house had become a take-no-prisoners zone that I returned to only to collect fresh clothes. To get by, I worked a series of classy jobs: insurance company file clerk; mail sorter at Oscar Mayer Wiener, Inc.; bookstore cashier. My safe house was there, in my friends' high-ceilinged, airy rooms scented with bayberry candles and fresh-cut lilacs in a hamlet outside the city with the winning Welsh name of Gwynnedd Valley. But then I was also in love, more or less, with the two other daughters of the house, and they with me, more or less. We somehow managed assignations at different times, sometimes on the same day, with no one any the wiser, we thought.

Pain kept me awake most nights, so I was usually there to catch my friend when he came home from the clubs, very stiff, in the deep A.M., and sat heavily on the kitchen floor, begging me to stay up with him because he had great new jokes to try out. He picked up his best gags in bars, he said. At a birthday party for his wife, where I was drunk and quite cunningly, I thought, wooing both sisters at once without either one knowing, they got into a hissy spat. She threw champagne in his face and ran from the house. He gave chase down a country lane, shouting so loudly that we all could hear. Come home. I'll be good. I'll change.

✡

Do faces belong to the body? Sometimes I have my doubts. They seem to lead independent lives, meeting each other unburdened by the rest of the body. Faces come directly from the demonic and form the angelic, from the depths and from the heights; the rest is merely terrestrial.

—Guido Ceronetti, *The Silence of the Body*

✡

The chunky stew of bar violence becomes in retrospect shockingly organized and clear. In my late teens one of my best friends was a Marine stationed at the naval base in Philadelphia who played drums in the band that performed weekends in the officers' club. One Saturday night, things felt off. You could sense trouble in the air like a smell rising from the compost of beer, sex, stifled expectations, and rage. After the first set, the lead guitar, a baby-faced lance corporal, was fuming. One of the officers had dressed him down and threatened harm if he didn't stop making eyes at the wife, which the guitarist swore he did not do, no sir. We tried to calm him. We knew he got into trouble without much trouble. "I don't care if he hits me," he said, showing us one side of his face, "because this is all plastic, I can't feel a thing." He'd had reconstructive surgery for the pulp of his face after a previous fight.

But he quieted down, the band played on, and everybody drank more while the women danced and laughed loudly. The band takes five, the guitarist, a smile on his remodeled face, puts down his instrument and steps off the dais toward a crowd of officers and wives seated at a table, picking up between here and there a wooden folding chair which, without a word, he axes down on the head and shoulders of one of them. Then there's disorder, women screaming, and the strip runs out there.

Eros—blissful confounding Eros—can be so soggy and bitter. It's sex and love. Or it's sex sniffing sex and nothing more. It can be practically anything we want it to be because, if we believe Jung, it's really a field of relatedness, me to tree and sisters to sea and pussy to prick and any permutation or elaboration of these. Eros energizes the relation of the living mind to its images of the dead. "Field of relatedness" makes it sound like a stable or stabilizing medium, but we don't experience it as an idea or paradigm; it *comes upon us* as bliss or woe, a rush, all blood, saliva, pulse, and thirst.

And our imagination is the excitable custodian of sensory memory. One night during the months I'd spent in a hospital bed because of the ailment that kept me awake on that sofa, a nurse I hadn't seen before visited, late, while I listened to Monk or Charles Lloyd or Morgana King on Philadelphia's great jazz station, WHAT. She told me I could stand if I really wanted to. That she would help. When with her support I got up on my pins, she turned her back to me, wrapped my arms around her waist, and snugged her butt against my groin. She hummed a little to the music, swayed just enough to rock my pain and make me hard, swayed protectively and invitingly with the young, mysteriously ruined white boy, who did his best to dance along. She said I seemed nice and promised, once I got well, to take me dancing. The slick crispness of her cotton tunic stretched taut across her belly down to her heavy-tissued thighs and ass. Such a gentle manner she had, and the background music hummed straight through her into my cock. The moment planted deep in me the certainty that no sexual experience could ever satisfy the way that killingly bittersweet flirtation did. In that moment I must have given up the rest of my life. (I thought, as a young man will, that I was going to die anyway from my undiagnosed ailment: the young man who shared my room died from bone cancer.) She drew me into another kind of disorder, of complete unmediated pleasure that asks nothing but that you give the rest of your life to it, to the moment of it. Bliss is always loss, and we remember both as one trembling movement of the spirit. Eros fulfills itself by exhausting itself, it enlivens the life it's draining. After that encounter, after that full-body promise of a real dance someday, my nurse never came back.

ACKNOWLEDGMENTS

Some of the material in this book appeared, in some form or other, in three previous, out-of-print collections: *Memory and Enthusiasm* (Princeton University Press); *Out of Eden* (University of California Press); and *Shooting the Works* (TriQuarterly Books). "Our Sweating Selves" first appeared in *The American Dante* (Farrar, Straus, and Giroux, 2001). "Late Arrivals" and miscellaneous material I've shanghaied from "*Semba!* A Notebook" for use in other essays first appeared in *Poetry*. My special thanks to two editors who have shown longtime loyalty and faith: Wendy Lesser of the *Threepenny Review* ("Fathead's Hard Times," "Hats," "Force," "Gots Is What You Got," "Make Me a Picture," "Inside the Box," "Unlovely Unlovable," "Ripe Fruit," "Nice Touch," "Your Show of Shows," and random bits from *Threepenny*'s "Table Talk" column that I've stitched into longer things here); and Jim Holman, editor of the *San Diego Reader*, who has given me such a free hand ("Love for Sale," "Stendhal Syndrome," "City Dog," "Rocking at the Cadillac," "Not Exactly a Self-Interview," and threads from columns I've written for his newspaper that I've woven into other, longish pieces here). And to Master Bill, *mille grazie*.